101 Math Activities

for Calculating Kids

Written by Tracey Ann Schofield

Illustrated by Alex Glikin

Teaching & Learning Company

1204 Buchanan St., P.O Box 10
Carthage, IL 62321-0010

9803875

This book belongs to

_____

Dedication

*This book is for every man, woman and child who has ever struggled with,
even hated, mathematics. Take heart. I am one of you.
And for my husband, Jonathan, my clever, occasionally fallible (but always sure of himself),
personal calculator. He keeps my checkbook and my life balanced.*

Special Thanks

*I wish to thank my husband, Jonathan, and my sons, Matthew and Patrick, for providing me with the hard data for many of the activities in this book; my daughter Stephanie for entertaining herself so wonderfully well while I hammered out "one last question" each day after school; Rob Ferguson and his grade 5 class at R.H. Cornish P.S. for taking the "Class Dribble Challenge" (twice!) and executing a splendid pen and pencil count; Rick Scragg and his grade 8 gifted class at R.H. Cornish P.S. for measuring up and joining the birthday club; Rob Johansen of S.A. Cawker P.S. for giving me the goods on his teaching staff; Dan Reid for kickstarting my dormant math memory; Coleen Power for lending me her library statistics; Heather Lang-Runtz for editing our magazine, **Long Term Care**, while I wrote this book; my mom for offering to type while I languished (and panicked) on the couch with a middle ear infection; and my dad, for just being my dad.*

I would also like to thank Inspiration, that wonderful creature of creative intervention that comes to me in my blankest hours with ideas worthy of publication. I would be lost without her.

Cover design by Peggy Larson

Copyright © 2001, Teaching & Learning Company

ISBN No. 1-57310-269-5

Printing No. 987654321

Teaching & Learning Company
1204 Buchanan St., P.O. Box 10
Carthage, IL 62321-0010

Table of Contents

Dear Teacher or Parent,

When I was first approached about writing a math book, I quailed at the prospect. Math was never my best subject. How was I to develop a book of 101 activities to help children plumb the murky depths of addition, subtraction, multiplication and division when I myself had struggled with these same subjects?

Mulling over my early and formative math years as I prepared to write this book, I came to understand that part of the reason I had never developed an appreciation for mathematics was that the subject had meant nothing to me personally. As a young student, I completed math exercises because they were required, not because they piqued my interest, appealed to my intellect or entertained me even remotely. Standard textbooks had failed completely to make math in any way relevant to my life. What interest did I have in Sally's apples and Jeff's oranges and the combined imaginary fruit total of these two strangers? Math exercises held no context; they offered nothing that would connect the required calculations and permutations to my immediate world and my small sphere of self-interest.

Having in retrospect grasped at least part of the problem, I developed *101 Math Activities for Calculating Kids* as a partial solution, creating a math book that is, I believe, unlike any other. Instead of Sally and Jeff, *101 Math Activities for Calculating Kids* puts every child who uses the book front and center, basing each and every math activity and question on his or her unique personal experience and circumstance. In writing a math book about each child's life history, I hope to have made an often tedious subject imminently more interesting, if not compelling.

101 Math Activities for Calculating Kids is a unique, student-directed approach to math practice that makes addition, subtraction, multiplication and division both fun and meaningful. Unlike standard math primers, there is no set answer to many of the questions in this book: each child will come to a different conclusion based on his or her personal experience and immediate environment. An answer key is provided to guide children through the calculations required to complete the 10 math questions in each activity.

I hope *101 Math Activities for Calculating Kids* helps your students to discover, enjoy and appreciate the math in their lives. I had great fun writing the book, and I made a late, great discovery while developing its 1010 questions: I like mathematics!

Sincerely,

Tracey

Tracey Ann Schofield

How to Use This Book

- Provide students with both the question and the answer key for each activity. Kids should be encouraged to use the answer key to check their methodology and to help them if they get stuck.

- Encourage kids to calculate by hand! Calculators should be used only when an activity demands calculations beyond the manual ability level of the child.

- As in the answer key, kids should show their calculations and write their answers in sentence form. (When a sentence starts with a number, children should be encouraged to write out the number and put the numeral form in brackets immediately following, i.e. "Sixty [60] percent of the paper clips are in the desk drawer." Numbers under 10 should be written out with the numeral form in brackets immediately following, i.e. "There are seven [7] paper clips in the drawer.")

- If a question or answer requires the use of whole numbers, kids should be directed to round to the nearest whole number.

- Children should be instructed to read through an entire activity before beginning to answer any of the 10 questions.

- Although certain of these activities might be beyond the ability level of some children, all children should be encouraged to attempt all activities. These activities are designed to challenge. By providing kids with an answer key for each activity, even those that are difficult can be successfully completed. Provided the child

has the raw data—which he or she will derive from his or her personal circumstances and environment—he or she should be able to complete the most demanding activities. Most kids will be able to work through a number of questions in each activity without referring to the answer key. At the very least, all kids should be able to gather the raw data required for each activity.

- This book provides kids with 101 self-directed math practice activities. Teachers and parents are encouraged to offer minimal assistance with calculations. Instead they should encourage kids to use the answer key and to work through difficult questions by example.

- Educators might ask one student to put his or her answers on the board at the completion of each activity. Teachers and students can then work through the example as a class, giving participants an opportunity to reconfirm their work.

Going Digital

Unlike the other activities in this book—which are subjective in nature and yield answers that vary according to the student's personal experience, interests and environment—the answers in this activity are the same for all students. This warm-up activity is intended to familiarize kids with the language, thought processes and types of calculations and written responses they will encounter and be expected to produce in the remaining 100 activities. Kids will not be able to check the accuracy of their answers in these activities, but instead will use the answer key to check the accuracy of the methodology used to derive those answers.

Draw the number keypad on your telephone.

1. Write the numbers on the keypad, from left to right, top to bottom, in numerical form. (What is this number in words?)
2. Add the numbers on the keypad together. What is the sum?
3. Multiply the numbers on the keypad together. (Treat the zero as a one.) What is the product?
4. Subtract each number on the keypad from your total in question 3. What is the difference?
5. Add the numbers on the X together. What is the sum?
6. Multiply the numbers on the X together. What is the product?
7. Subtract each number on the X from your multiplication total in question 6. What is the difference?
8. Add the numbers on the cross together. What is the sum?
9. Multiply the numbers on the cross together. (Treat the zero as a one.) What is the product?
10. Subtract each number on the cross from your multiplication total in question 9. What is the difference?

Design your own math question using the number keypad on your telephone. Make sure to do the calculations yourself and provide an answer key for your classmates.

Answer Key

```
1 2 3
4 5 6
7 8 9
* 0 #
```

1. The telephone keypad, expressed in numerical form from top to bottom and left to right, is 1,234,567,890. (In words, this number is one billion, two hundred thirty-four million, five hundred sixty-seven thousand, eight hundred ninety.)
2. Adding the numbers on the keypad together yields a sum of 45. [1 + 2 + 3 + 4 + 5 + 6 + 7 + 8 + 9 + 0 = 45]
3. Multiplying the numbers on the keypad together yields a product of 362,880. [$1 \times 2 \times 3 \times 4 \times 5 \times 6 \times 7 \times 8 \times 9 \times 1$ (substituted for 0) = 362,880]
4. Subtracting the numbers on the keypad from the total in question 3 yields a difference of 362,835. [362,880 - 1 - 2 - 3 - 4 - 5 - 6 - 7 - 8 - 9 - 0 (no substitution) = 362,835]
5. Adding the numbers on the "X," or diagonal, together yields a sum of 30. [1 + 5 + 9 + 3 + 5 + 7 = 30]
6. Multiplying the numbers on the "X," or diagonal, together yields a product of 4725. ($1 \times 5 \times 9 \times 3 \times 5 \times 7 = 4725$)
7. Subtracting the numbers on the "X," or diagonal, from the total in question 6 yields a difference of 4695. [4,725 - 1 - 5 - 9 - 3 - 5 - 7 = 4,695]
8. Adding the numbers on the "T," or cross, together yields a sum of 30. [2 + 5 + 8 + 0 + 4 + 5 + 6 = 30]
9. Multiplying the totals on the "T," or cross, together yields a product of 9600. [$2 \times 5 \times 8 \times 1$ (substituted for 0) $\times 4 \times 5 \times 6 = 9600$]
10. Subtracting the numbers on the "T," or cross, from the total in question 9 yields a difference of 9570. [9600 - 2 - 5 - 8 - 0 (no substitution) - 4 - 5 - 6 = 9570]

Things to Think About: How would the answers to questions 3 and 9 have changed if the number one had not been substituted for the zero? How would the answers to questions 3 and 9 have changed if the number 10 had been substituted for the zero? How could you have calculated the answers to questions 4, 7 and 10 using your answers from questions 2, 5 and 8? Why are the sums in questions 5 and 8 the same, while the products in questions 6 and 9 are different? Would it make any difference to your answers if you added, subtracted or multiplied the numbers on the telephone keypad in a different order?

Birthday Blitz

Determine the birth date of every member of your household.

1. Organize this list of dates according to years, from 1900 forward.

2. Organize this list of dates according to months, from January to December.

3. Organize this list of dates according to days from 1 to 31.

4. What is the mean year of birth of the members of your family?

5. What is the median year of birth of the members of your family?

6. What is the mean birth date of the month of the members of your family?

7. What is the median birth date of the month of the members of your family?

8. Express your birth date list in dd/mm/yy format. Express each of these as a number.

9. Add together the list of dd/mm/yy figures from question 8. What is the sum?

10. What is the mean of the numbers in question 8? (What is the median?)

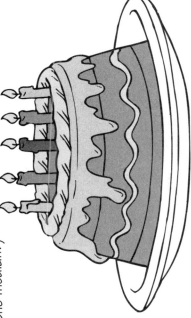

Answer Key

1. 1961, March 22nd (Jonathan); 1963, May 20th (Tracey); 1987, August 12th (Matthew); 1990, March 28th (Patrick); 1991, August 13th (Stephanie).

2. March 22, 1961 (Jonathan); March 28, 1990 (Patrick); May 20, 1963 (Tracey): August 12, 1987 (Matthew); August 13, 1991 (Stephanie).

3. 12th August, 1987 (Matthew); 13th August, 1991 (Stephanie); 20th May, 1963 (Tracey): 22nd March, 1961 (Jonathan); 28th March, 1990 (Patrick).

4. The mean year of birth of the members of my family is 1978. [1961 + 1963 + 1987 + 1990 + 1991 = 9892 (sum of birth years of family members) / 5 (family members) = 1978.4 = 1978]

5. The median, or middle year of birth, of my family members is 1987. [1991, 1990, <u>1987</u>, 1963, 1961. If there had been an even number of birth years, the median would have been half the sum of the two middle years.]

6. The mean birth date of the month of the members of my family is 19. [28 + 22 + 20 + 13 + 12 = 95. 95 (sum of birthdates of family members) / 5 (family members) = 19]

7. The median birth date of the months of the members of my family. [28, 22, <u>20</u>, 13, 12. If there had been an even number of birth dates, the median would have been half the sum of the two middle dates.]

8. 22/03/61 (Jonathan); 20/05/63 (Tracey); 12/08/87 (Matthew); 28/03/90 (Patrick); 13/08/91 (Stephanie). 220,361 (Jonathan); 200,563 (Tracey); 120,887 (Matthew); 280,390 (Patrick); 130,891 (Stephanie).

9. The sum of the dates in question 8 is 963,092. [220,361 + 200,563 + 120,887 + 280,390 + 130,891 = 953,092]

10. The mean of the numbers in question 8 is 190,618. (The median is 200,563.) [953,092 (sum of numbers) / 5 (numbers included in sum) = 190,618.4 = 190,618. 280,390; 220,361; 200,563; 130,891; 120,887]

Age Appropriate

Be an age detective.

1. In descending order, list the age of each member of your household.

2. What is the youngest age? What is the oldest age? What is the age difference between the youngest and the oldest?

3. How much older than the youngest are you? How much younger than the oldest are you?

4. If the oldest person in your household was seven years younger and the youngest person was seven years older, what would be the age difference between the youngest and the oldest?

5. Add the ages of the people in your household together. What is the combined age of the people in your household?

6. What is the average age of the people in your household?

7. How old is the family member who is closest in age to the average age of your household? How old is the family member who is furthest from the average age?

8. In ascending order, what are the ages of your grandparents (or what would they be if they were still alive)?

9. What is the average age of your grandparents?

10. If all of your grandparents were living at your house, what would be the average age of the members of your household?

Answer Key

1. The age list for the members of my household is, in descending order: Jonathan, 39; Tracey, 37; Matthew, 13; Patrick, 10; and Stephanie, 9.

2. The youngest age is nine (9). The oldest age is 39. The age difference between the youngest and the oldest is 30 years. [39 years (oldest, Jonathan) – 9 years (youngest, Stephanie) = 30 years].

3. I am 28 years older than the youngest and two (2) years younger than the oldest. [37 years (Tracey) – 9 years (Stephanie) = 28 years, 39 years (Jonathan) – 37 years (Tracey) = 2 years]

4. If the oldest person in my household was seven years younger and the youngest person was seven years older, the age difference between the youngest and the oldest would be 16 years. [39 years (Jonathan) – 7 years = 32 years. 9 years (Stephanie) + 7 years = 16. 32 years (Jonathan) – 16 years (Stephanie) = 16 years.

5. The combined age of the people in my household is 108 years. [39 + 37 + 13 + 10 + 9 = 108]

6. The average age of the people in my household is 22 years. [108 years (combined age) / 5 (number of people in household) = 22 years (rounded up from 21.6)]

7. The family member who is closest in age to the average age of my household is 13 years old. The family member who is furthest in age to the average age of my household is 39 years old.

8. In ascending order, my grandparents would be 85, 90, 94 and 96 years of age.

9. The average age of my grandparents would be 91. [85 + 90 + 94 + 96 = 365. 365 (combined age of grandparents) / 4 (number of grandparents) = 91 years (rounded down from 91.25)]

10. If all of my grandparents were living at my house, the average age of the members of my household would be 53 years. [108 years (combined age of Schofield household) + 365 years (combined ages of grandparents) = 473 years, 473 years (combined age of household with grandparents) / 9 (number of people in combined household) = 53 years (rounded up from 52.55)]

Twice Is Nice

1. In ascending order, list the age of each member of your household. Write the individual ages of your family in ascending order as a single number.
2. Double the number in question 1.
3. Express the number in question 1 in words.
4. Assign a place value to each number in question 1.
5. Rewrite your list from question 1 in descending order after doubling the age of each member of your household. Write the doubled individual ages of your family in descending order as a single number.
6. Double the number in question 5.
7. Write the number in question 5 in words. Assign a place value to each number in question 5.
8. Rewrite your list from question 1 in ascending order after halving the age of each member of your household. Write the halved individual ages of your family in ascending order as a single number.
9. Double the number in question 8.
10. Write the number in question 8 in words. Assign a place value to each number in question 8.

Answer Key

1. In ascending order, the ages of my family members are: Stephanie, 9; Patrick, 10; Matthew, 13; Tracey, 37; Jonathan, 39. Expressed as a single number: 910,133,739.
2. Doubling the number in question 1 yields a product of 1,820,267,478.
3. Expressed in words, the number in question 1 is: nine hundred ten million, one hundred thirty-three thousand, seven hundred thirty-nine.
4. The number in question 1 with place values assigned: 9 one hundred millions, 1 ten million, 0 millions, 1 hundred thousand, 3 ten thousands, 3 thousands, 7 hundreds, 3 tens, 9 ones.
5. The list from question 1, rewritten in descending order after doubling each age, is: Jonathan: 78; Tracey: 74; Matthew: 26; Patrick: 20; Stephanie: 18. Expressed as a single number: 7,874,262,018.
6. Doubling the number in question 5 yields a product of 15,748,524,036.
7. Expressed in words, the number in question 5: seven billion, eight hundred seventy-four million, two hundred sixty-two thousand, eighteen. The number in question 5 with place values assigned: 7 billions, 8 one hundred millions, 7 ten millions, 4 millions, 2 hundred thousands, 6 ten thousands, 2 thousands, 0 hundreds, 1 ten, 8 ones.
8. The list from question 1, rewritten in ascending order after halving each age: Stephanie: 4.5; Patrick: 5; Matthew: 6.5; Tracey: 18.5; Jonathan: 19.5. Expressed as a single number: 45,565,185,195.
9. Doubling the number in question 8 yields a product of 91,130,370,390.
10. Expressed in words, the number in question 8: forty-five billion, five hundred sixty-five million, one hundred eighty-five thousand, one hundred ninety-five. The number in question 8 with place values assigned: 4 ten billions, 5 billions, 5 one hundred millions, 6 ten millions, 5 millions, 1 hundred thousands, 8 ten thousands, 5 thousands, 1 hundreds, 9 tens, 5 ones.

Family Alphanumerics

Write an alphabet code as follows:
A = 1, B = 2, C = 3, D = 4 and so on.

1. Write your name in alphanumeric code (first and last).
2. If you add the letters of your full name together, what is your name total?
3. Write the names of each of your family members in alphanumeric code.
4. Add the letters of each of your family members' names together. What are the totals?
5. Write the name totals in ascending order.
6. Who has the highest name in your family? Who has the lowest? What is the difference between the highest and lowest names?
7. What is the average size of a name in your family?
8. Write the first name totals for each of your family members in descending order. Who has the highest first name? Who has the lowest?
9. What is the average size of a first name in your family?
10. What is the sum of your family name, or surname? Compare this to the surname totals of your classmates. Who has the highest surname? Who has the lowest? What is the difference between your surname and the highest and lowest surnames in your class?

Answer Key

1. 20,18,1,3,5,25 (Tracey) 19,3,8,15,6,9,5,12,4 (Schofield)
2. If I add the letters of my full name together, my name total is 153. [20 + 18 + 1 + 3 + 5 + 25 = 72. 19 + 3 + 8 + 15 + 6 + 9 + 5 + 12 + 4 = 81. 72 + 81 = 153]
3. 10,15,14,1,20,8,1,14 (Jonathan) 19,3,8,15,6,9,5,12,4 (Schofield); 13,1,20,20,8,5,23 (Matthew) 19,3,8,15,6,9,5,12,4 (Schofield); 16,1,20,18,9,3,11 (Patrick) 19,3,8,15,6,9,5,12,4 (Schofield); 19,20,5,16,8,1,14,9,5 (Stephanie) 19,3,8,15,6,9,5,12,4 (Schofield).
4. Jonathan = 164 [10 + 15 + 14 + 1 + 20 + 8 + 1 + 14 = 83 + 81 (Schofield) = 164]; Matthew = 171 [13 + 1 + 20 + 20 + 8 + 5 + 23 = 90 + 81 (Schofield) = 171]; Patrick = 159 [16 + 1 + 20 + 18 + 9 + 3 + 11 = 78 + 81 (Schofield) = 159]; Stephanie = 178 [19 + 20 + 5 + 16 + 8 + 1 + 14 + 9 + 5 = 97 + 81 (Schofield) = 178]
5. 153 (Tracey); 159 (Patrick); 164 (Jonathan); 171 (Matthew); 178 (Stephanie).
6. Stephanie has the highest name (178). I have the lowest name (153). There is a difference of 25 between the highest and lowest names. [178 - 153 = 25]
7. The average size of a name in my family is 165. [153 + 159 + 164 + 171 + 178 = 825. 825 (family name total) / 5 (number of people in family) = 165]
8. 97 (Stephanie); 90 (Matthew); 83 (Jonathan); 78 (Patrick); Tracey (72). Stephanie has the highest name (97). I have the lowest name (72).
9. The average size of a first name in my family is 84. [97 + 90 + 83 + 78 + 72 = 420. 420 (family first name total) / 5 (number of people in family) = 84]
10. The sum of my family name, or surname, is 81.

Activity 6

Ylimaf Sciremunahpla
(reverse Alphanumeric)

Write an alphabet code as follows:
A = 26, B = 25, C = 24, D = 23, etc.

1. Write your name in alphanumeric code (first and last).
2. If you add the letters of your full name together, what is your name total?
3. Write the names of each of your family members in alphanumeric code.
4. Add the letters of each of your family members' names together. What are the totals?
5. Write the name totals in ascending order.
6. Who has the highest name in your family? Who has the lowest? What is the difference between the highest and lowest names?
7. What is the average size of a name in your family?
8. Write the first name totals for each of your family members in descending order. Who has the highest first name? Who has the lowest?
9. What is the average size of a first name in your family, or surname?
10. What is the sum of your family name, or surname? Compare this to the surname totals of your classmates. Who has the highest surname? Who has the lowest? What is the difference between your surname and the highest and lowest surnames in your class?

Answer Key

1. 7,9,26,24,22, 2 (Tracey) 8,24,19,12,21,18,22,15,23 (Schofield)
2. My name total is 261. [7+9+26+24+22+2 = 90 (Tracey) 8 + 24 + 19 + 12 + 21 + 18 + 22 + 15 + 23 = 162 (Schofield). 90 + 162 = 252.]
3. 17,12,13,26,7,19,26,13 (Jonathan) 8,24,19,12,21,18,22,15,23 (Schofield); 14,26,7,7,19,22,4 (Matthew) 8,24,19,12,21,18,22,15,23 (Schofield); 11,26,7,9,18,24,16 (Patrick) 8,24,19,12,21,18,22,15,23 (Schofield); 8,7,22,11,19,26,13,18,22 (Stephanie) 8,24,19,12,21, 18,22,15,23 (Schofield).
4. Jonathan Schofield = 295 [17+12+13+26+7+19+26+13 (Jonathan) = 133 + 162 (Schofield) = 295]. Matthew Schofield = 261 [14+26+7+7+19+22+4 (Matthew) = 99 + 162 (Schofield) = 261]. Patrick Schofield = 273 [11 + 26 + 7+ 9 + 18 + 24 + 16 = 111 (Patrick) + 162 (Schofield) = 273]. Stephanie Schofield = 308 [8 + 7 + 22 + 11 + 19 + 26 + 13 + 18 + 22 = 146 + 162 (Schofield) = 308].
5. 252 (Tracey); 261 (Matthew); 273 (Patrick); 295 (Jonathan); 308 (Stephanie).
6. Stephanie has the highest name in my family (308). I have the lowest name in our family (252). The difference between the highest and lowest names is 56. [308 - 252 = 56]
7. The average size of a name in my family is 278. [252 + 261 + 273 + 295 + 308 = 1389. 1389 (family name sum) / 5 (number of people in family) = 278 (rounded up from 277.8)
8. 146 (Stephanie); 133 (Jonathan); 111 (Patrick); 99 (Matthew); 90 (Tracey). Stephanie has the highest first name. I have the lowest first name.
9. The average size of a first name in my family is 116. [146 + 133 + 111 + 99 + 90 = 579. 579 (family first name sum) / 5 (number of people in family) = 116 (rounded up from 115.8)]
10. The sum of my family name, or surname, is 162.

The Height of Your Day

With backs against the wall, use a tape measure to determine the height of each of your family members.

1. How tall are you? (Express in feet/inches and inches.)
2. How tall is each member of your family? (Express in feet/inches.) Who is the tallest? Who is the shortest?
3. Express your answers in question 2 in inches.
4. How tall would you be if you were half the height of the tallest member of your family? What if you were twice the height of the shortest member of your family? (Express in inches and feet/inches.)
5. Add together the heights of your family members. Standing one on top of the other, how tall would your family stand? (Express in feet/inches and inches.)
6. What is the average height of a member of your family?
7. Which family member's height is closest to the average?
8. How much difference is there between your height and the average height of a member of your family?
9. If you eliminate the tallest and the shortest members of your family, how does this affect the average height of a member of your family?
10. Compare your family height average to those of your classmates. Relatively speaking, whose family is the tallest? Whose family is the shortest?

Answer Key

1. I am 5'10" tall, or 70 inches tall. [5 (feet) x 12 (inches/foot) + 10 (extra inches) = 70 inches]
2. Jonathan is 5'11"; Matthew is 5'4"; Patrick is 5'1"; Stephanie is 4'5". Jonathan is the tallest (5'11"). Stephanie is the shortest (4'5").
3. Jonathan is 71 inches [5 (feet) x 12 (inches/foot) + 11 (extra inches) = 71 inches]; Matthew is 64 inches [5 (feet) x 12 (inches/foot) + 4 (extra inches) = 64 inches]; Patrick is 61 inches [5 (feet) x 12 (inches/foot) + 1 (extra inch) = 61 inches]; Stephanie is [4 (feet) x 12 (inches/foot) + 5 (extra inches) = 53 inches].
4. I would be 35.5 inches (or 2'11½") tall if I were half the height of Jonathan, the tallest member of my family. If I were twice the height of the shortest member of my family, Stephanie, I would be 26.5 inches (or 2'2½") tall.
5. Adding together the heights of my family members yields a sum of 319 inches. [71 (Jonathan) + 70 (Tracey) + 64 (Matthew) + 61 (Patrick) + 53 (Stephanie) = 319.] Standing one on top of the other we would stand 319 inches tall, or 26'7" tall! [319 / 12 = 26. 26 x 12 = 312. 319 - 312 = 7]
6. The average height of a person in my family is 63.8 inches, or 5'3 ²/₃", tall. [319 (total inches) / 5 (members in family) = 63.8 inches. 63.8 / 12 = 5.5 x 12 = 60. 63.8 - 60 = 3.8. ⁸/₁₂ = ²/₃]
7. Matthew's height of 64 inches is closest to the average of 63.8 inches.
8. The difference between my height and the average height of a member of my family is 6.2 inches. [70 inches (my height) - 63.8 inches (average family height) = 6.2 inches.]
9. If I eliminate the tallest and the shortest members of my family, the average height of a member of my family increases by 1.2 inches to 65 inches. [319 (family total) – 71 (Jonathan, tallest) – 53 (Stephanie, shortest) = 195. 195 inches (height total of remaining three family members) / 3 (members remaining) = 65 inches.]

TLC10269 Copyright © Teaching & Learning Company, Carthage, IL 62321-0010

Activity 8

Weight Watchers

1. How much do you weigh?
2. How much does each one of your family members weigh? (Arrange in descending order.)
3. What is the weight difference between the heaviest and lightest person in your family?
4. To whom are you closest in weight?
5. How much weight would you have to gain to weigh as much as the heaviest person in your family? How much weight would you have to lose to weigh as little as the lightest person in your family?
6. What is the mean weight of a person in your family?
7. Which family member's weight is closest to your mean family weight?
8. How tall are you? (Measure in inches.) How much do you weigh per inch?
9. Based on your height in question 7, how many inches per pound are you?
10. How old are you? How many pounds of weight do you carry for every year of growth?

Answer Key

1. I weigh 160 pounds.
2. Jonathan (174 pounds); Tracey (160 pounds); Matthew (93 pounds); Patrick (83 pounds); Stephanie (47 pounds).
3. The weight difference between the heaviest and lightest persons in my family is 127 pounds. [174 pounds (Jonathan) – 47 pounds (Stephanie) = 127 pounds]
4. I am closest in weight to my husband, Jonathan, who is 174 pounds. [174 pounds (closest over) – 160 (my weight) = 14 pounds. 160 (my weight) – 93 (closest under) = 67. 14<67]
5. I would have to gain 14 pounds to weigh as much as the heaviest person in my family (Jonathan, at 174 pounds). I would have to lose 113 pounds to weigh as little as the lightest person in my family. [174 pounds (weight of heaviest person) – 160 pounds (my weight) = 14 pounds. 160 pounds (my weight) – 47 pounds (weight of lightest person) = 113 pounds]
6. The mean weight of a person in my family is 111 pounds. [174 + 160 + 93 + 83 + 47 = 557 pounds. 557 pounds (family weight total) / 5 (family members) = 111.4 = 111 pounds]
7. Matthew's weight of 93 pounds is closest to our mean family weight. [160 pounds (closest weight over mean) – 111 pounds (mean) = 49 pounds. 111 (mean) – 93 (closest weight under mean) = 18 pounds.]
8. I weigh 160 pounds and stand 70 inches tall. Therefore, I weigh 2.29 pounds per inch. [160 pounds / 70 inches = 2.29 pounds/inch]
9. I stand 70 inches tall and weigh 160 pounds. Therefore, I am 0.44 inches per pound. [70 inches / 160 pounds = 0.44 inches/pound]
10. I weigh 160 pounds and I am 37 years old. Therefore, I carry 4.32 pounds of weight per year of growth. [160 pounds / 37 years = 4.32 pound/year]

Hair Today, Gone Tomorrow

You will need a brush or comb, a piece of paper (graph paper would be super), some cellophane tape and a ruler for this activity.

Draw a horizontal line across your paper, about one inch from the bottom. Draw a vertical line down the left-hand side of your paper about an inch from the edge. Make sure it intersects with the horizontal line. Now run the brush through your hair. Remove one strand of hair from the brush. Ask each member of your family to donate one strand of hair to your math cause.

Arrange the hairs from shortest to longest, leaving about an inch between each, with the shortest hair about one inch from the vertical line on your paper. Tape each hair to your paper so that the root of the hair (the little fleshy lump at the end of the hair where it was attached to the scalp) is resting on the horizontal line. Pull each hair straight and tape at the top.

1. Measure your strand of hair. How long is it?
2. Measure the strands of hair donated by your family. How long is each?
3. Whose hair is the longest? Whose hair is the shortest? How much longer is the longest hair than the shortest hair?
4. How much longer or shorter is your hair than the longest or shortest hair?
5. What is the combined length of your family's hair?
6. What is the mean length of your family's hair? How does your hair compare to your family average?
7. If your hair grows at the rate of about $1/4$ inch per month, how long has it taken you to grow your hair to its current length?
8. Assuming your hair grows at the rate stated in question 7, at what approximate date will your hair reach two inches in length if you it to $1/2$ inch in length today?
9. Assuming your hair grows at the rate stated in question 7 and that you do not cut your hair in the next 12 months, what length will your hair be one year from today?
10. Label your hair graph.

Answer Key

1. My strand of hair is $2^1/4$ inches long.
2. Jonathan's hair is $1^1/2$ inches long; Matthew's hair is one inch long; Patrick's hair is $1/2$ inch long; Stephanie's hair is 15 inches long.
3. Patrick's hair is the shortest. Stephanie's hair is the longest. Stephanie's hair is $14^1/2$ inches longer than Patrick's hair. [$^{15}/_1$ inches x $^2/_2 = ^{30}/_2$ (Stephanie's hair) $- ^1/_2$ (Patrick's hair) $= ^{29}/_2 = 14.5 = 14^1/2$]
4. My hair is $12^3/4$ inches shorter than Stephanie's hair [$^{15}/_1$ x $^4/_4 = ^{60}/_4$ (Stephanie's hair) $- ^9/_4$ (my hair) $= ^{51}/_4 = 12.75 = 12^3/4$ inches] and $1^3/4$ inches longer than Patrick's hair [$^9/_4$ (my hair) $- ^2/_4$ (Patrick's hair) $= ^7/_4 = 1.75 = 1^3/4$ inches]
5. The combined length of my family's hair is $20^1/4$ inches long. [$^9/_4$ (my hair) $+ ^6/_4$ (Jonathan's hair) $+ ^4/_4$ (Matthew's hair) $+ ^2/_4$ (Patrick's hair) $+ ^{60}/_4$ (Stephanie's hair) $= ^{81}/_4 = 20.25 = 20^1/4$ inches
6. The mean length of my family's hair is 4 inches. [20.25 (family's hair lengths combined) / 5 (family members) $= 4.05 = 4.1 = 4$ inches.] My hair is $1^3/4$ inches shorter than our family average. [$^4/_1$ x $^4/_4 = ^{16}/_4$ (average) $- ^9/_4 = ^7/_4 = 1.75 = 1^3/4$ inches]
7. At a growth rate of $1/4$ inch per month, it has taken me nine (9) months to grow my hair to its current length. [$^9/_4$ (current length) / $^1/_4 = ^9/_4$ x $^4/_1 = ^{36}/_4 = 9$]
8. Assuming my hair grows at the rate $1/4$ inch per month, my hair will reach two inches in length on April 2nd, if I cut it to $1/2$ inch today. [$^2/_1$ x $^4/_4 = ^8/_4$ (two inches). $^1/_2$ x $^2/_2 = ^2/_4$ ($1/2$ inch today). $^8/_4 - ^2/_4 = ^6/_4 = 1.5 = 1^1/2$ (inches to grow). $^6/_4$ (to grow) / $^1/_4$ (growth/month) $= ^6/_4$ x $^4/_1 = 6$ months. Today is October 2. Six months from now it will be April 2.
9. Assuming my hair grows at $1/4$ inch per month and that I do not cut my hair in the next 12 months, my hair will be $5^1/4$ inches long one year from today. [$^1/_4$ inches/month x $^{12}/_1$ months $= 3$ inches/year. $2^1/4$ inches (today) $+ 3$ inches $= 5^1/4$ inches]
10. See graph.

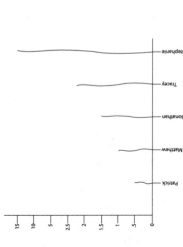

Waist Reduction

Assuming that size and age are equivalent, use the following chart to answer the questions in this activity.

Size/Age	Waist	Size/Age	Waist
1	19½	8	23
2	20	10	24
3	20½	12	25
4	21	14	26
5	21½	16	27
6	22	18	28
7	22½	20	29

1. Put this information on a graph with size on the vertical axis and waist on the horizontal axis. Extend the graph to age 30 and add these new coordinates to the size chart.

2. What is your age-to-waist measurement ratio?

3. How much larger is your waist measurement number than your age number?

4. What size will your waist be 13 years from now?

5. How much larger is your waistline today than it was when you were one (1)?

6. By how many inches will your waistline change over the next five years?

7. How big are the waistlines of your siblings? (If you don't have any siblings, imagine that you have a brother who is three years older and a sister who is three years younger than you.)

8. If waist size were to increase by ½ inch two years after age 30, ½ inch every 5 years after age 50 and ½ inch every 10 years after age 80, what is the waist measurement of each of your family members?

9. Based on the assumptions in question 8, how large will your waistline be 100 years from now?

10. What is your actual waist measurement? (Your waist is the indented area above your hips. Try bending to the side to find the natural indent. Use a tape measure to measure your waist at its narrowest point.) According to your waist measurement, how old are you?

Answer Key

1. See graph.

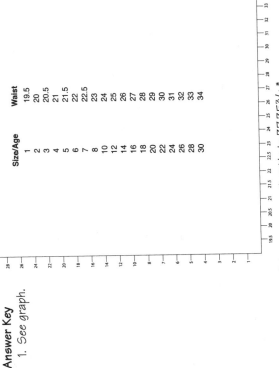

Size/Age	Waist
1	19.5
2	20
3	20.5
4	21
5	21.5
6	22
7	22.5
8	23
10	24
12	25
14	26
16	27
18	28
20	29
22	30
24	31
26	32
28	33
30	34

2. My age to waist measurement ratio is 37:35³/4.

3. My waist measurement number is 1¼ smaller than my age number. [37 - 35.75 = 1.25 = 1¼]

4. My current waist measurement is 35³/4. Thirteen years from now my waist measurement will be [37 years (current age) + 13 years = 50 years. 39 inches = 50 years]

5. My waistline is 16¼ more than it was when I was one (1). [35³/4 - 19¹/2 = 16¹/4]

6. Over the next five years my waistline will change by 1¹/4 inches from 35³/4 to 37 inches. [After 30, waist increases by ¹/2 inch every two years, or by ¹/4 inch every year and 1 inch every four years. I am currently 37. I will gain ¹/4 inch every year for five years. Therefore I will gain 1¹/4 inches over the next five years. 35³/4 inches (current waist) + 1¹/4 inches (additional) = 37 inches.]

7. My brother is 35. His waistline is 35¹/4.

8. Based on the assumptions set out in this question, my family members are: Jonathan (39 years): 36¹/4; Matthew (13): 25 ¹/2; Patrick (10): 24; Stephanie (9): 23¹/2.

9. One hundred years from now, my waistline will be 44¹/2 inches.

10. My actual waist measurement is 34 inches. According to my waist measurement, I am 30 years old.

*Because I am over 30 years of age, I am using the assumptions in question 8 for my calculations. Because students must extrapolate to find the over 30 age:waist coordinates, I am not showing most of my calculations.

Keyboard Computering

Draw the computer keyboard (letters only).

Assign each letter a number. The number at the far left of each row will be 1. Number up from 1 across each row.

1. Use the letter/number coordinates to find the sum of your name (first and last only).

2. Calculate the sums of the names of each of your family members. Who has the highest name total?

3. Add the sums of each family name together. What is your family total?

4. What is your family name average?

5. Subtract the highest and lowest totals from your family sum. By how much does your family total decrease? How does this affect your family average?

6. Subtract the name totals for the oldest and youngest members of your family. How does this affect your family total decrease? By how much does your family average?

7. Multiply together the numbers in your first name. Multiply together the numbers in your last name. Add these two products together. What is the sum?

8. Double the number values associated with each letter. Multiply together the numbers in your first name. Multiply together the numbers in your last name. Add these two products together. What is your new name product?

9. Divide your answers in questions 7 and 8 by the number of letters in your name. What are the quotients?

10. Compare your personal and family name totals to the personal and family name totals of your classmates. Who has the highest name total? Who has the lowest? Who has the highest/lowest average?

Answer Key

Q = 1 W = 2 E = 3 R = 4 T = 5 Y = 6 U = 7 I = 8 O = 9 P = 10
A = 1 S = 2 D = 3 F = 4 G = 5 H = 6 J = 7 K = 8 L = 9
Z = 1 X = 2 C = 3 V = 4 B = 5 N = 6 M = 7

1. Using the letter/number coordinates above, the sum of my name is 69. [[T = 5 + R = 4 + A = 1 + C = 3 + E = 3 + Y = 6] + (S = 2 + C = 3 + H = 6 + O = 9 + F = 4 + I = 8 + E = 3 + L = 9 + D = 3) = (22) + (47) = 69]

2. The sums of each of my family members' names are: 88 (Jonathan); 76 (Matthew); 86 (Patrick); and 91 (Stephanie). Stephanie has the highest name total (91). [J = 7 + O = 9 + N = 6 + A = 1 + T = 5 + H = 6 + A = 1 + N = 6 = 41 + 47 (for SCHOFIELD from question 1) = 88. M = 7 + A = 1 + T = 5 + T = 5 + H = 6 + E = 3 + W = 2 = 29 + 47 = 76. P = 10 + A = 1 + T = 5 + R = 4 + I = 8 + C = 3 + K = 8 = 39 + 47 = 86. S = 2 + T = 5 + E = 3 + P = 10 + H = 6 + A = 1 + N = 6 + I = 8 + E = 3 = 44 + 47 = 91]

3. My family name total is 410. [69 (Tracey) + 88 (Jonathan) + 76 (Matthew) + 86 (Patrick) + 91 (Stephanie) = 410]

4. My family name average is 82. [410 (family name total) / 5 (number of people in my family) = 82]

5. By subtracting the highest and lowest totals from my family sum, our family total drops by 177 [91 + 86] from 410 to 263. [410 - 91 = 319 - 86 = 233] How does this affect your family average? My family average actually increases to 88 from 82 in question 4. [233 (excluding highest and lowest totals) / 3 (number of family members remaining in calculation) = 77.6 = 78]

6. Subtracting the name totals for the oldest and youngest members of my family yields a new total of 231, which represents a decrease of 179. [410 - 88 (Jonathan) - 91 (Stephanie) = 231] [88 + 91 = 179] This yields a new family average of 77, which is lower than our average of 82 in question 4. [231 (excluding oldest and youngest family members) / 3 (number of family members remaining in calculation) = 77]

7. Multiplying together the letter/number coordinates in my first and last names and adding the two products together yields a total of 840,888. [[T = 5 × R = 4 × A = 1 × C = 3 × E = 3 × Y = 6] + (S = 2 × C = 3 × H = 6 × O = 9 × F = 4 × I = 8 × E = 3 × L = 6) + (S = 2 × C = 3 × H = 6 × O = 9 × F = 4 × I = 8 × E = 3 × L = 9 × D = 3) = (1080) + (839808) = 840,888]

8. Multiplying together the numbers in my first and last name and adding the two products together after doubling the letter values in both names yields a total of 430,050,816. [[T = 10 × R = 8 × A = 2 × C = 6 × E = 6 × Y = 12] + (S = 4 × C = 6 × H = 12 × O = 18 × F = 8 × I = 16 × E = 6 × L = 18 × D = 6) = (69,120) + (429,981,696) = 430,050,816]

9. Dividing my answer in question 7 by the number of letters in my name yields a quotient of 56,059. [840,888 (total in question 7) / 15 (number of letters in my name) = 56,059.2 = 56,059] Dividing my answer in my name yields a quotient of 28,670,054. [430,050,816 (total in question 8) / 15 (number of letters in my name) = 28,670,054.4 = 28,670,054]

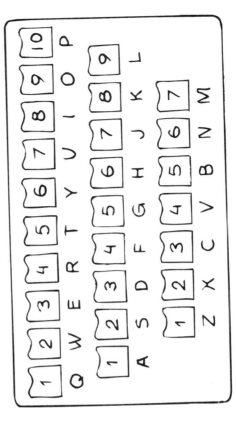

```
Q  W  E  R  T  Y  U  I  O  P
1  2  3  4  5  6  7  8  9  10

A  S  D  F  G  H  J  K  L
1  2  3  4  5  6  7  8  9

Z  X  C  V  B  N  M
1  2  3  4  5  6  7
```

The Handy Family

Get a blank piece of paper and colored pencils. Put the wrist of your left hand (right hand if you are left-handed) at the bottom edge of the paper. With fingers slightly apart, draw around the outline of your hand.

Ask your family members to let you trace their hands on the same piece of paper using a different colored pencil. (Make sure each person puts his or her wrist at the bottom edge of the piece of paper.)

Use your handprint graph to complete the questions in this activity.

1. Which of your fingers is the longest? How long is it? (Measure from the base of the finger, not the wrist.) How much longer is this finger than your second longest finger?
2. Measure the longest finger of each member of your family.
3. Who has the longest finger? How much longer is this finger than your longest finger? (If your finger is the longest, how much longer is your finger than the next longest finger in your family?)
4. Which of your fingers is the shortest? (Remember, your thumb is not a finger!) How long (or short!) is it? How much shorter is this finger than your longest finger?
5. Measure the shortest finger of each member of your family.
6. Who has the shortest finger? How much shorter is this finger than your shortest finger? (If your finger is the shortest, how much shorter is your finger than the next shortest finger in your family?)
7. Measure the thumb of each member of your family.
8. Who has the longest thumb in your family? How much longer is this thumb than your thumb? (If your thumb is the longest, how much longer is it than the next longest thumb in your family?)
9. Add the lengths of all your fingers. What is your total finger length?
10. Measure the hand width of each of your family members. (Measure at the widest point.) Who has the widest hand in your family? How wide is it? How much wider is the widest hand in your family than your hand? (If your hand is the widest, how much wider is it than the most slender hand in your family?)

Answer Key

1. My middle finger is the longest. It is $3\frac{1}{2}$ inches long. My middle finger is $\frac{1}{4}$ inch longer than my second longest finger, which is $3\frac{1}{4}$ inches long. $[3\frac{2}{4} - 3\frac{1}{4} = \frac{1}{4}]$
2. The longest fingers of each member of my family measure: $3\frac{3}{4}$ (Jonathan); $3\frac{1}{2}$ (Tracey); $3\frac{1}{4}$ (Matthew); 3 (Patrick); $2\frac{3}{4}$ (Stephanie).
3. Jonathan has the longest finger. Jonathan's finger is $\frac{1}{4}$ inch longer than my longest finger. $[3\frac{3}{4}$ (Jonathan) - $3\frac{2}{4}$ (mine) = $\frac{1}{4}]$
4. My baby finger is the shortest. It is $2\frac{1}{2}$ inches long. It is one (1) inch shorter than my longest finger. $[3\frac{1}{2} - 2\frac{1}{2} = 1]$
5. The shortest fingers of each member of my family measure: $2\frac{1}{2}$ (Jonathan); $2\frac{1}{2}$ (Tracey); $2\frac{1}{4}$ (Matthew); 2 (Patrick); $1\frac{3}{4}$ (Stephanie).
6. Stephanie has the shortest finger. Her shortest finger is $\frac{3}{4}$ inch shorter than my shortest finger: $[2\frac{1}{2} = 10/4, \ 1\frac{3}{4} = 7/4, \ 10/4$ (my shortest) - $7/4$ (Stephanie's shortest) = $3/4]$
7. The thumbs of each member of my family measure: 2 (Jonathan); 2 (Tracey); 2 (Matthew); $1\frac{3}{4}$ (Patrick); $1\frac{1}{2}$ (Stephanie).
8. Jonathan, Matthew and I are tied for first place in the longest thumb competition. Our thumbs each measure two (2) inches. Our thumbs are $\frac{1}{4}$ inch longer than Patrick's thumb, which is the next longest thumb in our family at $1\frac{1}{4}$ inches. $[8/4 - 7/4 = \frac{1}{4}]$
9. My total finger length, including my thumb, is $14\frac{1}{4}$ inches. $[2\frac{1}{2} + 3\frac{1}{4} + 3\frac{1}{2} + 3 + 2 = 14\frac{1}{4}]$
10. The hand widths of each member of my family measure: $4\frac{3}{8}$ (Jonathan); $3\frac{7}{8}$ (Tracey); $4\frac{1}{8}$ (Matthew); $3\frac{1}{2}$ (Patrick); $3\frac{1}{8}$ (Stephanie). Jonathan has the widest hand in our family. His hand is $\frac{1}{2}$ inch wider than my hand. $[4\frac{3}{8} - 3\frac{7}{8} = 3\frac{5}{8} - 3\frac{1}{8} = 4/8 = \frac{1}{2}]$

Activity 13

Fancy Footwork

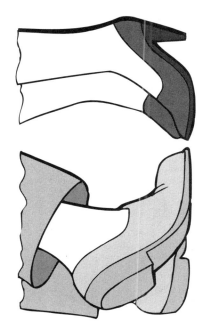

Use the chart below to complete the questions in this activity.

Foot Length	Shoe Size	Foot Length	Shoe Size
4 1/2	4	9 7/8	7 1/2
4 13/16	5	10	8
5 3/16	6	10 1/8	8 1/2
5 7/16	7	10 5/16	9
5 13/16	8	10 1/2	9 1/2
6 1/8	9	10 11/16	10
6 1/2	10	10 13/16	10 1/2
6 13/16	11	10	11
7 3/16	12	11 3/16	11 1/2
7 1/2	13	11 15/16	12
7 13/16	1	11 1/2	12 1/2
8 1/8	2	11 5/8	13
8 1/2	3	11 7/8	13 1/2
8 13/16	4	10	14
9 3/16	5	12 1/8	14 1/2
9 1/2	6	12 5/18	15
9 5/8	7		

Put your bare left heel at the bottom edge of a blank piece of paper. Trace your foot with a colored pencil. Using a measuring tape or ruler, record the length of your foot. Write your name and the length of your foot beside your footprint. Ask each member of your family to allow you to trace the outline of his

or her foot on the same piece of paper. (Make sure everyone puts his or her heel at the bottom edge of the paper and try to use different colored pencils.) Record the lengths of each foot and the owner of each footprint on your paper.

1. Record the foot length of each family member.
2. How much bigger is the biggest foot than the smallest foot?
3. What is the total foot length of your family?
4. What is the mean length of a foot in your family? How does your foot compare to the average foot in your family?
5. Using the chart, determine your shoe size by your foot length.
6. What is the shoe size of each member of your family?
7. What is the mean adult shoe size of a member of your family?
8. How does your shoe size compare to the average shoe size of a member of your family?
9. If your foot grows two inches, what size shoe will you need?
10. If your foot were one inch shorter, what size shoe would you need?

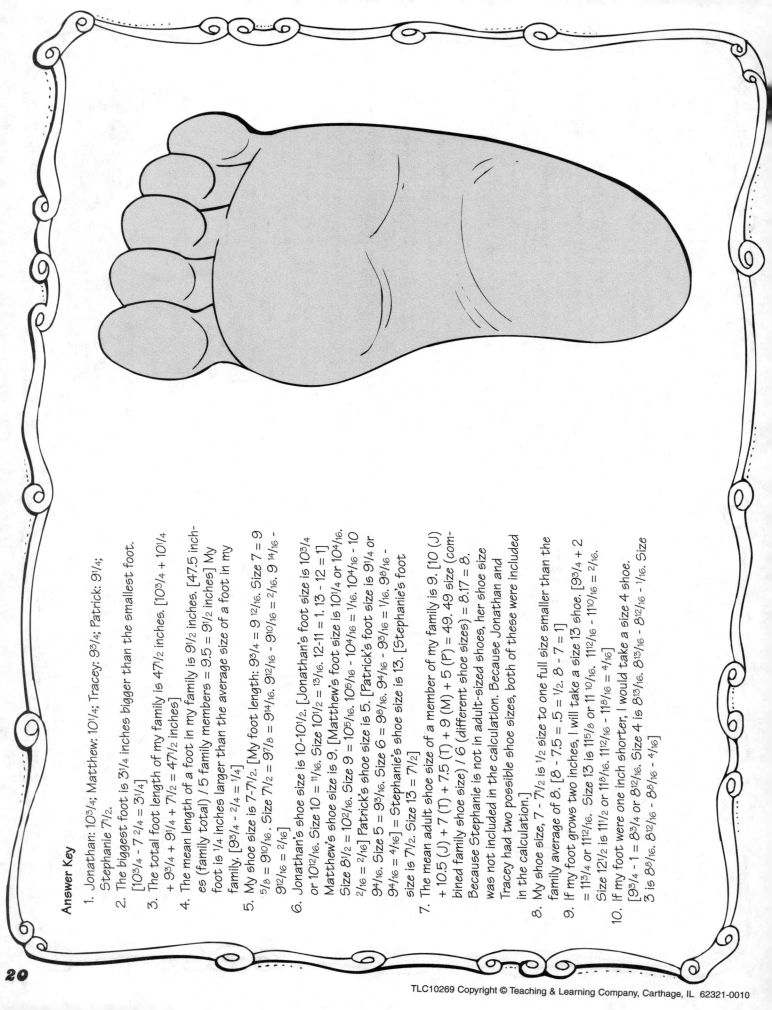

Answer Key

1. Jonathan: 10³/₄; Matthew: 10¹/₄; Tracey: 9³/₄; Patrick: 9¹/₄; Stephanie 7¹/₂.

2. The biggest foot is 3¹/₄ inches bigger than the smallest foot. [10³/₄ - 7 ²/₄ = 3¹/₄]

3. The total foot length of my family is 47¹/₂ inches. [10³/₄ + 10¹/₄ + 9³/₄ + 9¹/₄ + 7¹/₂ = 47¹/₂ inches]

4. The mean length of a foot in my family is 9¹/₂ inches. [47.5 inches (family total) / 5 family members = 9.5 = 9¹/₂ inches] My foot is ¹/₄ inches larger than the average size of a foot in my family. [9³/₄ - 2¹/₄ = ¹/₄]

5. My shoe size is 7-7¹/₂. [My foot length: 9³/₄ = 9 ¹²/₁₆. Size 7 = 9 ⁵/₈ = 9¹⁰/₁₆. Size 7¹/₂ = 9⁷/₈ = 9¹⁴/₁₆. 9¹²/₁₆ - 9¹⁰/₁₆ = ²/₁₆. 9 ¹⁴/₁₆ - 9¹²/₁₆ = ²/₁₆]

6. Jonathan's shoe size is 10-10¹/₂. [Jonathan's foot size is 10³/₄ or 10¹²/₁₆. Size 10 = ¹¹/₁₆. Size 10¹/₂ = ¹³/₁₆. 12-11 = 1. 13 - 12 = 1] Matthew's shoe size is 9. [Matthew's foot size is 10¹/₄ or 10⁴/₁₆. Size 8¹/₂ = 10²/₁₆. Size 9 = 10⁵/₁₆. 10⁵/₁₆ - 10⁴/₁₆ = ¹/₁₆. 10⁴/₁₆ - 10 ²/₁₆ = ²/₁₆] Patrick's shoe size is 9¹/₄ or 9⁴/₁₆. Size 5 = 9³/₁₆. Size 6 = 9⁸/₁₆. 9⁴/₁₆ - 9³/₁₆ = ¹/₁₆. 9⁸/₁₆ - 9⁴/₁₆ = ⁴/₁₆] = Stephanie's foot size is 7¹/₂. Size 13 = 7¹/₂] Patrick's shoe size is 5. [Patrick's shoe size is 5. Size 13. [Stephanie's foot size is 7¹/₂]

7. The mean adult shoe size of a member of my family is 9. [10 (J) + 10.5 (J) + 7.5 (T) + 9 (M) + 5 (P) = 49. 49 size (combined family shoe size) / 6 (different shoe sizes) = 8.17 = 8. Because Stephanie is not in adult-sized shoes, her shoe size was not included in the calculation. Because Jonathan and Tracey had two possible shoe sizes, both of these were included in the calculation.]

8. My shoe size, 7 - 7¹/₂ is ¹/₂ size to one full size smaller than the family average of 8. [8 - 7.5 = .5 = ¹/₂. 8 - 7 = 1]

9. If my foot grows two inches, I will take a size 13 shoe. [9³/₄ + 2 = 11³/₄ or 11¹²/₁₆. Size 13 is 11⁵/₈ or 11 ¹⁰/₁₆. 11¹²/₁₆ - 11¹⁰/₁₆ = ²/₁₆. Size 12¹/₂ is 11¹/₂ or 11⁸/₁₆. 11¹²/₁₆ - 11⁸/₁₆ = ⁴/₁₆]

10. If my foot were one inch shorter, I would take a size 4 shoe. [9³/₄ - 1 = 8³/₄ or 8¹²/₁₆. Size 4 is 8¹³/₁₆. 8¹³/₁₆ - 8¹²/₁₆ - ¹/₁₆. Size 3 is 8⁸/₁₆. 8¹²/₁₆ - 8⁸/₁₆ - ⁴/₁₆]

Everything's Relative

How many parents do you have? How many brothers and sisters do you have? How many nieces and nephews do you have? How many grandparents do you have? How many aunts, uncles and cousins do you have?

1. List your family figures.
2. Put your family figures in a chart in ascending order under the headings Number and Relations.
3. Of what relation do you have the most?
4. Of what relation do you have the least?
5. How many relatives do you have in total?
6. How many of your relatives are older than you?
7. How many of your relatives are younger than you?
8. How many of your relatives are the same age as you?
9. How many of your aunts/uncles/cousins are on your mother's side? How many are on your father's side? Whose side has more relations? How many more relatives does the one side have than the other?
10. Plot the information from your Family Figures Chart in question 2 on a graph with Number on the vertical axis and Relations on the horizontal axis.

Answer Key

1. Parents, 2; Grandparents, 4 (deceased); Brothers/brothers-in-law, 3; Sisters/sisters-in-law, 3; nieces, 2; nephews 2; aunts, 5 (two deceased); uncles, 4 (two deceased); cousins, 12.

2.

Number	Relations
2	Parents
2	Nieces
2	Nephews
3	Brothers/Brothers-in-Law
3	Sisters/Sisters-in-Law
4	Grandparents
4	Uncles
5	Aunts
12	Cousins

3. I have the most cousins.
4. I have the least parents, nieces and nephews.
5. I have 37 relatives in total. [2 + 2 + 2 + 3 + 3 + 4 + 4 + 5 + 12 = 37]
6. Twenty-one (21) of my relatives are older than I am. [2 (parents) + 1 (brother-in-law) + 1 (sister-in-law) + 4 (grandparents) + 4 (uncles) + 5 (aunts) + 4 (cousins) = 21]
7. Fourteen (14) of my relatives are younger than I am. [2 (nieces) + 2 (nephews) + 1 (brothers) + 1 (sister-in-law) + 8 (cousins) = 14]
8. Two (2) of my relatives are the same age as me. [1 (brother-in-law) + 1 (sister-in-law) = 2]
9. One (1) of my aunts, one (1) of my uncles and (2) of my cousins are on my mother's side. Four (4) of my aunts, three (3) of my uncles and 10 of my cousins are on my father's side. My father's side has 13 more relations than my mother's side. [1 + 1 + 2 = 4 (mother's side). 4 + 3 + 10 = 17 (father's side). 17 - 4 = 13]
10. See graph.

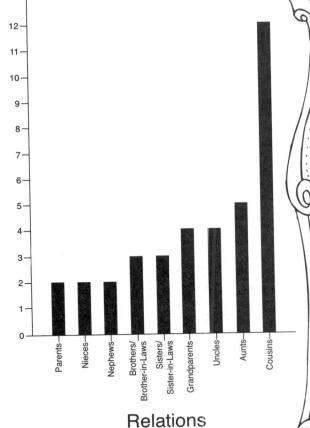

Numbers

(bar graph: Parents 2, Nieces 2, Nephews 2, Brothers/Brother-in-Laws 3, Sisters/Sister-in-Laws 3, Grandparents 4, Uncles 4, Aunts 5, Cousins 12)

Relations

Relatively Speaking

Find out the birthdays the members of your immediate and extended family.

1. Record the birthdays (including your own).
2. Write the birthday month information from question 1 in a chart under the headings *Number of Birthdays* and *Month*.
3. How many of your relatives share your birthday month?
4. Which month has the most birthdays? Which month(s) has (have) the least?
5. In which months were your grandparents born?
6. How many birthdays are on each date? How many relatives share your birth date?
7. Put the birth day information from question 6 in chart under the headings *Number of Birthdays* and *Birth Date*.
8. Which date has the most birthdays?
9. Considering the calendar year, which relative's birthday is furthest from yours? Which is closest to yours?
10. Write the information from question 2 on a graph with *Number of Birthdays* on the vertical axis and *Month* on the horizontal axis. Put the information from question 7 on a graph with *Number of Birthdays* on the vertical axis and *Birth Date* on the horizontal axis.

Answer Key

1. **My Immediate/Extended Family Birthday List**

January: Bet (27th)

February: Derek (14th), Angela (23rd)

March: Connor (6th), Lorraine (8th), Linda (13th), Jono (22nd), Patrick (28th)

April: Grandpa C. (6th), Mary Lou (17th), Bob (19th), Grandpa G. (20th)

May: Jennifer (14th), Linda (15th), Tracey (20th), Ryan (22nd)

June: Grandma C. (6th), Kelley (9th), Meghan (20th)

July: Bryan (7th), Grandma G. (10th), Scott (17th), Graeme (18th), Matt (21st)

August: Beryle (1st), Barb (9th), Cameron (10th), Mattie (12th), Stephie (13th), Penny (14th), Pat (22nd), Taylor (27th)

September:

October: Michael (20th), Rhianna (22nd)

November: Valerie (26th), Maureen (29th)

December: Paul (6th), Kerri (20)

2. 1-January, 2-February, 5-March, 4-April, 4-May, 3-June, 5-July, 8-August, 0-September, 2-October, 2-November, 2-December,

3. Three (3) of my relatives share my birthday month, which is May: my sisters-in-law Jennifer and Linda and my nephew Ryan.

4. August has the most birthdays in it (8). September has the least (0).

5. My grandfathers were both born in April. One of my grandmothers was born in June. The other was born in July.

6. 1st = 1; 6th = 4; 7th =1; 8th = 1; 9th = 2; 10th = 2; 12th = 1; 13th = 2; 14th = 3; 15th = 1; 17th = 2; 18th = 1; 19th = 1; 20th = 5; 21st = 1; 22 = 4; 23rd = 1; 26th = 1; 27th = 2; 28th = 1; 29th = 1.

7. 1-1, 4-6, 1-7, 1-8, 2-9, 2-10, 1-12, 2-13, 3-14, 1-15, 2-17, 1-18, 1-19, 5-20, 1-21, 4-22, 1-23, 1-26, 2-27, 1-28, 1-29.

8. The 20th has the most birthdays—5.

9. Considering the calendar year, my niece Kerri's birthday, which is on the 20th of December, is furthest from mine. My nephew Ryan's birthday, which is on the 22nd of May, is nearest to mine.

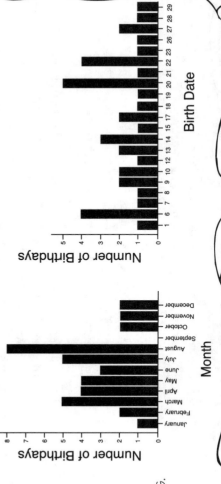

Activity 16

I'm Alive!

Write the date of your birth.

1. How many years old are you?
2. Express your age in months.
3. Express your age in weeks. (Round to the nearest week.)
4. Express your age in days.
5. How many hours have you been alive? (Round to the nearest hour.)
6. How many minutes have you been alive? (Round to the nearest minute.)
7. Express your age in years, months, days, hours and minutes. (Remember, a new day begins at midnight, or 12:00 a.m.)
8. How many days old were you at the turn of the century (January 1, 2000)?
9. How many hours will you have been alive on your next birthday?
10. How many minutes will you have been alive when school ends this year?

Answer Key

May 20, 1963

1. I am 37 years old.
2. I am 448 months old. [37 (years) x 12 (months/year) = 444 + 4 months (May-Sept) = 448]
3. I am 1942 weeks old. [37 (years) x 52 (weeks/year) = 1924 + 18 weeks (May 20-Sept 16) = 1942]
4. I am 13,640 days old. [37 (years) x 365 (days/year) = 13,505 + 9 days (due to leap year - add one extra day every four years - 37/4 = 9.25 or 9) = 13,514 + 126 days (18 weeks May 20-Sept 16 x 7 days/week) = 13,640]
5. I have been alive for 327,346 hours. [13,640 (days) x 24 (hours/day) = 327,360 - 14 hours (because it is only 10:15 a.m. on my 13,622nd full day of my life) = 327,346]
6. I have been alive for 19,614,855 minutes. [327,346 (hours) x 60 (minutes/hour) = 19,640,760 - 840 (It is only the 10th hour of the day which is 14 hours x 60 minutes/hour less than the full minute count for the day) = 19,639,920 minutes + 15 minutes (it is 15 minutes past the hour) = 19,639,935]
7. The time is 10:15 a.m. I have been alive for 37 years, 126 days, 327,346 hours and 15 minutes.
8. September 16 is 260 days (Jan = 31days + Feb = 29 + March = 31 + April = 30 + May = 31 + June = 30 + July = 31 + August = 31 + September=16 = 260 days) into the new century. I was 13,380 days old on January 1, 2000. [13,640 (days old today) - 260 (days since January 1) = 13,380.
9. On my next birthday, I will have been alive for 332,880 hours. [38 (years old) x 365 (days/year) = 13,870 days x 24 (hours/day) = 332,880]
10. When this school year finishes, I will be 20,028,390 minutes old. [Last day of school is June 28, 2001. Dismissal time is 2:30 p.m. Therefore: 13,909 (days old as of June 28, 2001) x 24 (hours/day) = 333,816 x 60 (mins/hour) = 20,028,960 minutes - 570 minutes (9 hours, 30 minutes {9 x 60 = 540 + 30 = 570} from full 24 hour count) = 20,028,390]

In the Blink of an Eye

Count the number of times you blink in one minute. (Repeat this exercise five times.)

If one of your blink counts is much higher or lower than the rest, delete it and complete one more trial.)

1. How many times did you blink in each one-minute trial?
2. What is your average number of blinks per minute?
3. Based on your answer to question 2, this represents one blink every how many seconds? (In other words, how many seconds are there between each blink?)
4. Based on your answer to question 2, how many times do you blink in an hour?
5. How many times do you blink in a day? (Remember, you don't blink in your sleep!)
6. How many times do you blink in a week?
7. How many times do you blink in a year?
8. If you live to be 75 years of age, approximately how many times will you blink in your lifetime?
9. If your eyes start getting dry when you turn 65, and you have to blink twice as often, how many times will you blink if you live to be 100?
10. If you slept 16 hours a day for the first four (4) years of your life, how many times did you blink in your first 10 years?

Answer Key

1. I blinked 16, 13, 17 14 and 18 times in my five one-minute trials.
2. My average number of blinks per minute is [16 + 13 + 17 + 14 + 18 = 78 (combined blinks/minute) / 5 (number of trials) = 16 blinks/minute (rounded up from 15.6)
3. I blinked once every 3.75 seconds. [60 (seconds/min) / 16 (blinks/min) = 3.75 seconds]
4. I blink 960 times per hour. [16 (blinks/minute) x 60 (mins/hour) = 960 (blinks/hour)]
5. I blink in a day. [24 (hours/day) - 8 (hours sleep/day) = 16 hours. 960 (blinks/hour) x 16 (hours/day) = 15,360 (blinks/day)]
6. I blink 107,520 times per week. [15,360 (blinks/day) x 7 (days/week) = 107,520 (blinks/week)]
7. I blink 5,591,040 times per year. [107,520 (blinks/week) x 52 (weeks/year) = 5,591,040 (blinks/year)]
8. If I live to be 75 years of age, I will blink 419,328,000 in my lifetime. [5,591,040 (blinks/year) x 75 years = 419,328,000 (blinks in 75 years)]
9. If my eyes start getting dry when I turn 65, and I have to blink twice as often, I will blink 754,790,400 times if I live to be 100 years of age. [419,328,000 (blinks in 75 years) - 55,910,400 (blinks in 10 years) = 363,417,600 (blinks in 65 years) (OR: 5,591,040 (blinks/year) x 65 (years) = 363,417,600). 5,591,040 (blinks/year) x 2 = 11,820,080 (blinks/year) x 35 years = 391,372,800 (blinks in 35 years). 363,417,600 (blinks in 65 years) + 391,372,800 (blinks in 35 years) = 754,790,400 (blinks in 100 years)]
10. If I slept 16 hours a day for the first four (4) years of my life, I would blink 44,728,320 times in my first 10 years. [24 (hours/day) - 16 (hours sleep/day) = 8 (awake hours). 960 (blinks/hour) x 8 (awake hours/day) x 7 (days/week) x 52 (weeks/year) x 4 (years) = 11,182,080 (blinks in 4 years). 5,591,040 (blinks/year) x 6 (years) = 33,546,240 (blinks in 6 years). 11,182,080 (blinks in 4 years) + 33,546,240 (blinks in 6 years) = 44,728,320 (blinks in 10 years)]

Activity 18

Counting, Counting, 1, 2, 3

You will need a watch or timer for this counting activity.

1. Counting out loud and starting at one (1), how high can you count in a one-minute period? (No shortcuts! You have to say the full name of each number. And no slurring! Each number must be recognizable when you say it.)

2. Based on your total in question 1, how high should you be able to count in two minutes?

3. Based on your total in question 1, how high should you be able to count in five minutes?

4. Counting out loud and starting at one (1) again, how high can you count in two minutes? Is your estimate correct?

5. Counting out loud and starting at one (1) again, how high can you count in five minutes? Is your estimate correct?

6. What is the difference between your estimate in question 2 and your total in question 4? How much less was your counting total than your estimate?

7. What is the difference between your estimate in question 3 and your total in question 5? How much less was your counting total than your estimate?

8. What is happening? Why are your answers to questions 2 and 3 different from your answers in questions 4 and 5?

9. Compare your words/minute counts for one, two and five minutes. What is happening to your words/minute count?

10. If you lived to be 100 and you started counting today, could you count to a million in your lifetime? (Justify your answer.)

Answer Key

1. I counted to 144 in one minute.

2. Based on my total in question 1, I should be able to count to 288 in two minutes. [144 × 2 = 288]

3. Based on my total in question 1, I should be able to count to 720 in five minutes. [144 × 5 = 720]

4. I can count to 214 in two minutes. My estimate is wrong.

5. I can count to 399 in five minutes. My estimate is wrong.

6. The difference between my estimate in question 2 and my total in question 4 is 74. [288 - 214 = 74] My counting total is 74 numbers less than my estimate.

7. The difference between my estimate in Question #3 and my total in question 5 is 321. [720 - 399 = 321] My counting total is 321 numbers less than my estimate.

8. My estimates are falling increasingly further out of line with my actual counting ability. (Why?)

9. I counted 144 words/minute in one minute; 107 words/minute in two minutes [214 (total words counted) / 2 (minutes) = 107 (words/minute)]; and 80 words/minute in five minutes [399 (total words counted) / 5 (minutes) = 80 (rounded up from 79.8)] My words/minute count is dropping as the time increases. (Why?)

10. Answers and justifications will vary.

Here's to Your Hoppiness

1. How many times in a row can you hop on your right foot? (Stop counting as soon as your left foot touches the ground or you have to grab onto something to regain your balance or you get to tired to continue!) Try two more hopping trials on your right foot.

2. How many right foot hops did you do in total?

3. What is your average number of right foot hops over the three trials?

4. How many times in a row can you hop on your left foot? Try two more hopping trials on your left foot.

5. How many left foot hops did you do in total?

6. What is your average number of left foot hops over the three trials?

7. On which foot did you do the greatest number of hops in a single trial? How many more hops is this than your best hop on the other foot?

8. On which foot did you do the least number of hops in a single trial? How many fewer hops is this than your worst hop on the other foot?

9. How does your right foot hop total compare to your left foot hop total?

10. How does your right foot hop average compare to your left foot hop average?

Answer Key

1. I hopped 134 times in a row in my first right foot trial. I hopped 95 and 111 times a row in my second and third right foot trials respectively.

2. I did 340 right foot hops in total. [134 + 95 + 111 = 340]

3. My average number of right foot hops over the three trial is 113. [340 right foot hops (total over three trials) / 3 trials = 113.3 = 113]

4. I hopped 129 times in a row in my first left foot trial. I hopped 107 and 114 times in a row in my second and third left foot trials respectively.

5. I did 350 left foot hops in total. [129 + 107 + 114 = 350]

6. My average number of left foot hops over the three trials is 117. [350 left foot hops (total over three trials) / 3 trials = 116.6 = 117]

7. I did the greatest number of hops in a single trial on my right foot: 134. This is 5 hops more than my best hop on my left foot. [134 (best right) – 129 (best left) = 5.]

8. I did the least number of hops in a single trial on my right foot: 95. This is 12 fewer hops than my worst hop on my left foot. [107 (worst left) – 95 (worst right) = 12.]

9. My right foot hop total of 340 is 10 less than my left foot hop total of 350. [350 (left) – 340 (right) = 10.]

10. My right foot hop average of 113 is 4 less than my left foot average of 117. [117 (left foot average) – 113 (right foot average) = 4]

Activity 20

Present Products

Think about your dream birthday

1. If everyone close to you–friends and family–gave you a birthday gift, how many presents would you receive?

2. If, for your birthday, each of your family members gave you two gifts and each of your close friends gave you one gift, how many presents would you receive?

3. If each of the family members in question 1 had given you a present since your first birthday, how many gifts would you have received from this group of people in total?

4. If each of the friends in question 1 gives you a birthday gift from this day forward, how many presents will you receive from this group of people by the time you are 25?

5. If you sent a thank-you card or made a phone call of appreciation to each person in question 1 once every five years, how many messages of thanks would you deliver in 25 years?

6. If you gave each person in question 1 a gift for his or her birthday, how many gifts would you give in three years?

7. If you gave gifts to only half of the people in question 1, how many gifts would you give in eight years?

8. If each of the gifts in question 6 cost $11.50, how much money would you spend in the three years?

9. If you had a birthday party, how many people would you invite? If, instead of a gift, each person attending your party donated $12.50 to your favorite charity, how much money would be raised in your name?

10. If, instead of a gift, each of the family members in question 1 gave $15 to your favorite charity, how much money would be raised in your name? Add this to the money raised in question 9. How much charity birthday money would be raised in your name by the people in these two groups? (Don't worry if some of the people in the two groups overlap.) If this tradition continued from your last birthday until your 25th birthday, how much money would be raised in your name in total?

Answer Key

1. If everyone close to me–friends and family– gave me a birthday gift, I would receive 15 presents. [10 gifts from family members + 5 gifts from close friends = 15 gifts]

2. If, for my birthday, each of my family members gave me two gifts and each of my close friends gave me one gift, I would receive 25 presents. [10 x 2 (family) = 20; 5 x 1 (friends) = 5; 20 + 5 = 25]

3. If each of the family members in question 1 had given me a present since my first birthday, I would have received 555 gifts from this group of people in total. [15 people x 37 birthdays = 555 gifts]

4. If each of the friends in question 1 gives me a birthday gift from this day forward, I will receive 65 presents from this group of people by the time I am 50. (Since I am over 25, I changed this figure to 50.) [50 (projected age) - 37 (current age) = 13. 13 birthdays x 5 friends = 65]

5. If I sent a thank-you card or made a phone call of appreciation to each person in question 1 once every five years, I would deliver 75 messages of thanks in 25 years. [5 messages of thanks x 15 people = 75]

6. If I gave each person in question 1 a gift for his or birthday, I would give 45 gifts in three years. [15 gifts x 3 years =45]

7. If I gave gifts to only half of the people in question 1, I would give 8 gifts in 8 years. [15 people / 2 = 7.5 = 8; 8 gifts x 8 years = 64 gifts]

8. If each of the gifts in question 6 cost $11.50, I would spend $517.50 in the three years. [45 x $11.50 = $517.50]

9. If I had a birthday party, I would invite 21 people. If instead of a gift, each person attending my party donated $12.50 to my favorite charity, $262.50 would be raised in my name. [21 guests x $12.50/guest = $262.50]

10. If, instead of a gift, each of the family members in question 1 gave $15 to my favorite charity, $150 would be raised in my name. [10 x 15 = $150] When I add this to the donation in question 9, the people in these two groups would raise $412.50 in charity birthday money in my name. [$262.50 party + $150 family = $412.50.] If this tradition continued from my last birthday until my 50th birthday, $5362.50 would be raised in my name in total. (Because I am over 25, I changed the projected age to 50.) [50 (projected age) - 37 (current age) = 13. $412.50 each year x 13 years = $5362.50]

Keep it Up

Blow up a balloon or a beach ball. Ask a friend or family member to play a short game of "Keep it Up" with you.

1. Take turns hitting the balloon back and forth to each other. How many times can you hit the balloon between you before it touches down? (The object is to keep the balloon in the air for as long as possible. When the balloon touches anything other than a body part or when someone hits the balloon twice in a row, the round is over.)

2. Play four more rounds of "Keep it Up." How many hits did the two of you score in each round?

3. How many hits did you score in total over the five rounds?

4. What is your average score over the five rounds?

5. What was the median (middle) score of the five rounds?

6. What was your highest score? What was your lowest score? What is the difference between your highest and lowest scores?

7. For what percentage of the total hits does your best round account?

8. For what percentage of the total hits does your worst round account?

9. If you hit the ball twice as well in your best three rounds, what would be your hit total over the five rounds? How would this affect your five round hit average?

10. If you hit the ball twice as well in your worst three rounds, what would be your hit total over the five rounds? How would this affect your five round hit average?

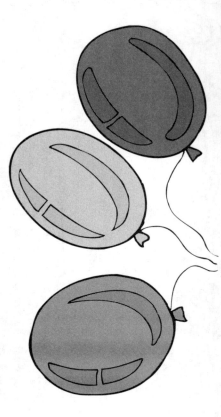

Answer Key

1. We hit the balloon 13 times in the first round of "Keep it Up."

2. We hit the ball 16, 5, 20 and 12 times in the next four rounds respectively.

3. We scored 66 hits in total over the five rounds. [13 + 16 + 5 + 20 + 12 = 66]

4. Our average score over the five rounds was 13 hits. [66 hits / 5 rounds = 13.2 = 13 hits/round]

5. Our median (or middle) score of the five rounds was 13 hits. [20, 16, 13, 12, 5]

6. Our highest score was 20. Our lowest score was 5. The difference between our highest and lowest scores was 15. [20 - 5 = 15]

7. Our best round accounts for 30 percent of our hit total. [20 hits (best round) / 66 hits (total) x 100 = 30.3 = 30%]

8. Our worst round accounts for 8 percent of our hit total. [5 hits (worst round) / 66 hits (total) x 100 = 7.6 = 8%]

9. If we hit the ball twice as well in our best three rounds, our hit total over the five rounds would be 115. [20 x 2 = 40. 16 x 2 = 32. 13 x 2 = 26. 40 + 32 + 26 + 12 + 5 = 115] This would increase our five round hit average by 10 from 13 to 23. [115 hits (total) / 5 rounds = 23 hits/round. 23 (new average) - 13 (old average) = 10]

10. If we hit the ball twice as well in our worst three rounds, our hit total over the five rounds would be 96. [13 x 2 = 26. 12 x 2 = 24. 5 x 2 = 10. 20 + 16 + 26 + 24 + 10 = 96.] This would increase our five round hit average by 6 from 13 to 19. [96 hits (total) / 5 rounds = 19.2 = 19 hits/round. 19 (new average) - 13 (old average) = 6]

Activity 22

Stayin' Up Alone

Try playing solo "Keep it Up" or "Stayin' Up Alone."
Bounce the balloon or beach ball with
any body part but your hands and arms.

1. Play a round of "Stayin' Up Alone." How many bumps did you score before ending the round? (The round ends when you touch the balloon with your hands or arms or when the balloon touches anything other than an approved body part.) Play four more rounds of "Stayin' Up Alone." What were your scores in these four rounds?

2. How many times did you bump the ball in total over the five rounds?

3. What is your average score over the five rounds?

4. What was the median (middle) score of the five rounds?

5. What was your highest number of bumps in a single round? What was your lowest number of bumps in a single round? What was the difference between your highest number of bumps and your lowest number of bumps?

6. Ask your friend to complete five rounds of "Stayin' Up Alone." What are his or her scores?

7. How many times did your friend bump the ball in total?

8. What is your friend's average score over the five rounds?

9. Over the five rounds, was your average score higher or was your friends' average score higher? How much higher was the higher average score than the lower average score?

10. Who had the highest number of bumps in a single round? How much higher was this total than the other person's highest single round bump total?

Answer Key

1. My scores over five rounds of "Stayin' Up Alone" were 8, 10, 7, 9 and 11.

2. I bumped the ball 45 times in total over the five rounds. [8 + 10 + 7 + 9 + 11 = 45]

3. My average score over the five rounds was 9. [45 bumps total / 5 rounds = 9]

4. The median (middle) score of the five rounds was 9. [11, 10, 9, 8, 7. Median = 9]

5. My highest number of hits in a single round was 11. My lowest number of hits in a single round was 7. The difference between my highest number of hits and my lowest number of hits is 4. [11 - 7 = 4.]

6. My friend's scores over five rounds of "Stayin' Up Alone" were 5, 6, 5, 8 and 5.

7. My friend bumped the ball 29 times in total. [5 + 6 + 5 + 8 + 5 = 29]

8. My friend's average score over the five rounds was 6. [29 bumps total / 5 rounds = 5.8 = 6]

9. My average score of nine (9) bumps was three (3) bumps higher than my friends' average score of six (6) bumps.

10. I had the highest number of bumps in a single round. My highest round bump total of 11 bumps was 3 bumps higher than my friend's highest single round bump total of 8. [11 - 8 = 3]

Toothy Tallies

Open your mouth and look in a mirror at your teeth.

1. How many teeth do you have?
2. How many teeth are on your upper jaw? How many teeth are on your lower jaw?
3. If you lost nine (9) teeth, four from the upper and five from the lower, how many would you have left in total? How many on the upper and lower jaws?
4. How many molars do you have? What is the ratio of molars to other teeth in your mouth?
5. What percentage of your teeth are molars?
6. How many fillings can you see in your mouth?
7. What is the ratio of teeth without fillings to teeth with fillings?
8. What percentage of your teeth have fillings?
9. If you went to the dentist and he or she filled three more cavities, what percentage of your teeth would have fillings?
10. If the dentist filled three teeth every two years, how many years would it take until every tooth in your mouth had a filling?

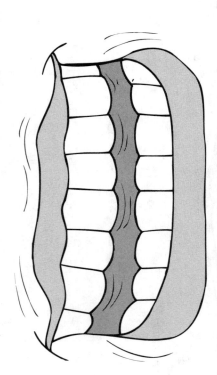

Answer Key

1. I have 28 teeth.
2. I have 14 teeth on the upper jaw and 14 teeth on the lower jaw.
3. If I lost nine (9) teeth, I would have 19 teeth remaining, 10 on the upper jaw and nine (9) on the lower jaw. [28 (teeth in total) - 9 (teeth lost) = 19. 14 (upper teeth) - 4 (lost teeth) = 10 (teeth remaining). 14 (lower teeth) - 5 (teeth lost) = 9 (teeth remaining)]
4. I have 16 molars. The ratio of molars to other teeth in my mouth is 16:12 or 4:3. [$^{16}/_4 = 4 : ^{12}/_4 = 3$]
5. Fifty-seven percent of my teeth are molars. [16 (molars) / 28 (total teeth) x 100 = 57.14 = 57%]
6. I can see 11 fillings in my mouth.
7. The ratio of teeth without fillings to teeth with fillings is 17:11. [28 (total teeth) - 11 (teeth with fillings) = 17 (teeth without fillings)]
8. Thirty-nine percent of my teeth have fillings. [11 (teeth with fillings) / 28 (total teeth) x 100 = 39.28 = 39%]
9. If I went to the dentist and he filled three more cavities, 50 percent of my teeth would have fillings. [11 (teeth with fillings) + 3 (additional cavities) = 14 (teeth with cavities. 14 (teeth with fillings) / 28 (total teeth) x 100 = 50%]
10. If the dentist filled three teeth every two years, it would take 12 years until every tooth in my mouth had a filling. [28 (teeth total) - 11 (teeth with fillings) = 17 (teeth without fillings. 3 fillings in 2 years; 6 in 4; 9 in 6; 12 in 8; 15 in 10; 18 fillings in 12 years]

Activity 24

Functions with Fluids

Track your fluid intake for one day.

1. Assuming one regular glass holds 8 ounces of fluid (and one trip to the water fountain counts as one glass of water), how many glasses of fluid did you drink?

2. How many ounces of fluid did you drink in one day?

3. What kinds of fluid did you drink? List each type, with number of glasses, in ascending order.

4. What is your favorite fluid? How many ounces of this fluid did you drink?

5. If you doubled your daily intake of your favorite fluid, how many ounces of this fluid would you drink in a week?

6. If you drank twice as much of your first fluid, three times as much of your second fluid, four times as much of your third fluid, etc., how much fluid in total would you consume in one day?

7. How many glasses of fluid did you drink at each meal (credit your "in-between" fluid intake to your meal balance: between breakfast and lunch is added to lunch; between lunch and dinner is added to lunch; between dinner and bedtime is added to dinner).

8. On average, how many glasses of liquid did you have with each meal?

9. If you drank twice as much at breakfast, half as much at lunch and three times as much at dinner, how much fluid would you drink?

10. If your weekend fluid consumption rate is twice that of your weekday rate, how much fluid would you drink in a month?

Answer Key

1. I drank 12 glasses of fluid.

2. I drank 96 ounces of fluid. [12 (glasses) × 8 (ounces/glass) = 96 (ounces of fluid)]

3. I drank one (1) glass of cola, three (3) glasses of milk and eight (8) glasses of water.

4. My favorite fluid is water. I drank 64 ounces of this fluid. [8 (glasses of water) × 8 (ounces/glass) = 64 ounces of water.

5. If I doubled my daily intake of water, my favorite fluid, I would drink 896 ounces of this fluid in a week. [64 (ounces daily) × 2 = 128 ounces/day. 128 (ounces/day) × 7 (days/week) = 896 (ounces/week)]

6. If I drank twice as much of my first fluid, three times as much of my second fluid and four times as much of my third fluid, I would consume 344 ounces of fluid in one day. [1 (glass) × 2 = 2. 3 (glasses) × 3 = 9. 8 (glasses) × 4 = 32. 2 (glasses) + 9 (glasses) + 32 (glasses) = 43 (glasses). 43 (glasses of fluid) × 8 (ounces/glass) = 344 (ounces/day)]

7. I drank three (3) glasses at breakfast; five (5) glasses at lunch; and four (4) glasses at dinner.

8. On average, I had four (4) glasses of fluid with each meal. [3 (glasses, breakfast) + 5 (glasses, lunch) + 4 (glasses, dinner) = 12 (glasses, total). 12 (glasses, total) / 3 (meals) = 4 (glasses/meal)]

9. If I drank twice as much at breakfast, half as much at lunch and three times as much at dinner, I would drink 20.5 glasses of fluid in one day. [2 × 3 (glasses, breakfast) = 6. ½ × 5 (glasses, lunch) = 2.5. 3 × 4 (glasses, dinner) = 12. 6 + 2.5 + 12 = 20.5]

10. If I drank twice as much on weekends as I did on weekdays, I would drink 3456 ounces of fluid in a month. [12 glasses (weekday) × 5 (days/week) × 4 (weeks/month) = 240 (glasses weekdays). 12 (glasses/weekday) × 2 × 4 (Saturdays/month)= 96. 12 (glasses/weekday) × 2 × 4 (Sundays/month) = 96 (glasses). 240 + 96 + 96 = 432 (glasses/month). 432 (glasses/month) × 8 ounces/glass) = 3456 (ounces/month)]

Activity 25

Solo Dribbler

For this activity you will need a basketball, a watch or clock, a piece of paper, and a pencil or pen. (If you don't have a basketball at home, you might have to do this exercise at school.)

1. Time yourself for one minute. See how many times you can dribble (or bounce) the basketball in that one-minute period. (If you "fumble" mid-dribble, recover the ball as quickly as possible and continue.) What was your one-minute dribble count?

2. Try four more dribble trials. What was your dribble count for each trial?

3. What was your highest dribble count? What was your lowest dribble count? What was the difference between your highest and lowest dribble counts?

4. How many times did you dribble the ball in total over your five dribble trials?

5. What was your average dribble count over the five trials?

6. How much higher was your highest dribble count than your dribble average?

7. How much lower was your lowest dribble count than your dribble average?

8. If you eliminate your highest and lowest dribble counts, how does this affect your dribble average?

9. What is the median (middle) dribble count of the five dribble trials?

10. How does the median dribble count compare to your dribble count average? How does the median dribble count compare to your modified dribble count average in question 9?

Answer Key

1. I dribbled the ball 157 times in my one-minute dribble trial.

2. My dribble counts for each of four more trials were: 215, 205, 195 and 226.

3. My highest dribble count was 226. My lowest dribble count was 157. The difference between my highest and lowest dribble counts was 69. [226 (highest) - 157 (lowest) = 69]

4. In total, I dribbled the ball 998 times over my five dribble trials. [157 + 215 + 205 + 195 + 226 = 998.]

5. My average dribble count over the five dribble trials was 200. [998 dribbles / 5 trials = 199.6 = 200 dribbles/trial.]

6. My highest dribble count of 226 was 26 dribbles higher than my average dribble count of 200. [226 (highest) - 200 (average) = 26.]

7. My lowest dribble count of 157 dribbles was 43 dribbles lower than my average dribble count of 200. [200 (highest) - 157 (lowest) = 43.]

8. If I eliminate my highest and lowest dribble counts, my dribble count average increases by five (5) dribbles from 200 to 205. [998 - 226 - 157 = 615. 615 dribbles / 3 trials = 205 dribbles/trial.]

9. The median (middle) dribble count of the five dribble trials is 205. [226, 215, 205, 195, 157.]

10. The median dribble count of 205 is five (5) dribbles higher than my average dribble count of 200. [205 median - 200 average = 5.] The median dribble count is the same as the modified dribble count in question 9. [205 = 205.]

Activity 26

Toy Story

Group the toys in your bedroom or toy room according to the following classifications: stuffed, plastic, metal, wooden, foam. (If you have too many toys to count in a few minutes, estimate. If you do not have any toys in your room, use your imagination. Pretend that your room is filled with the toys of your dreams, and use these dream toys in your calculations. If you don't feel very imaginative, you could ask a friend to let you take an inventory of his or her toy collection.)

1. How many toys do you have in each category?
2. Which category has the most toys? Which category has the least toys? How many more toys are in the most popular category than the least popular category?
3. How many toys do you have in total?
4. What percent of the total number of toys are in the stuffed category? Express the number of stuffed toys as a fraction of the whole. What is the ratio of stuffed to plastic toys?
5. What percent of the total number of toys are in the plastic category? Express the number of plastic toys as a fraction of the whole. What is the ratio of plastic to metal toys?
6. What percent of the total number of toys are in the metal category? Express the number of metal toys as a fraction of the whole. What is the ratio of metal to wooden toys?
7. What percent of the total number of toys are in the wooden category? Express the number of wooden toys as a fraction of the whole. What is the ratio of wooden to foam toys?
8. What percent of the total number of toys are in the foam category? Express the number of foam toys as a fraction of the whole. What is the ratio of foam to stuffed toys?
9. If you had 1/4 the number of toys, how many toys would you have? If you had 1/4 fewer toys, how many toys would you have?
10. If you had four times the number of toys, how many toys would you have? How many more toys would you have?

Answer Key

1. My kids have approximately 275 stuffed, 550 plastic, 75 metal, 25 wooden, 6 foam toys.

2. The plastic category is the largest with 550 toys. The foam category is the smallest with six (6) toys. My kids have 544 more plastic toys than foam toys. [550 (plastic) - 6 (foam) = 544.]

3. In total, my kids have approximately 931 toys. [275 + 550 + 75 + 25 + 6 = 931]

4. Thirty (30) percent of the total number of toys are in the stuffed category. [275 stuffed toys / 931 toys total x 100 = 29.5 = 30%] The number of stuffed toys expressed as a fraction of the whole is 275/931. The ratio of stuffed to plastic toys is 1:2. [275:550. 275 / 275 = 1. 550 / 275 = 2. 1:2]

5. Fifty-nine (59) percent of the total number of toys are in the plastic category. [550 plastic toys / 931 toys total x 100 = 59.1 = 59%] The number of plastic toys expressed as a fraction of the whole is 550/931. The ratio of plastic to metal toys is 22:3. [550:75. 550 / 25 = 22. 75 / 25 = 3]

6. Eight (8) percent of the total number of toys are in the metal category. [75 metal toys / 931 toys total x 100 = 8.1 = 8%] The number of metal toys expressed as a fraction of the whole is 75/931. The ratio of metal to wooden toys is 3:1. [75:25. 75/25 = 3. 25/25 = 1. 3:1]

7. Three (3) percent of the total number of toys are in the wooden category. [25 wooden toys / 931 toys total x 100 = 2.7 = 3%.] The number of wooden toys expressed as a fraction of the whole is 25/931. The ratio of wooden to foam toys is 25:6.

8. One (1) percent of the total number of toys are in the foam category. [6 foam toys / 931 toys total x 100 = 0.6 = 1%] The number of foam toys expressed as a fraction of the whole is 6/931. The ratio of foam to stuffed toys is 6:275.

9. If my kids had 1/4 the number of toys, they would have 233 toys. [931 x 1/4 = 232.75 = 233] If they had 1/4 fewer toys, they would have 698 toys. [931 - 233 = 698]

10. If my kids had four times the number of toys, they would have 3724 toys. [931 x 4 = 3724] They would have 2793 more toys. [3724 - 931 = 2793]

Shootin' Hoops

For this activity you will need a basketball and net (or a scrunched up piece of paper and a wastepaper basket).

1. Stand 5 paces (long walking strides) back from the net. Throw the ball 10 times. How many baskets did you score in your 10 throws? Try two more trials of 10. How many baskets did you score in each trial?

2. How many baskets did you score in total over your three trials? What is your ratio of baskets scored to shots taken? Describe this ratio in terms of baskets scored for every shot taken. Express your shooting accuracy in this repetition as a percentage.

3. What is your average score per trial over the three trials?

4. Stand 10 paces back from the net. Execute three trials of 10 throws each. How many baskets did you score in each trial?

5. How many baskets did you score in total over your three trials? What is your ratio of baskets scored to shots taken? Describe this ratio in terms of baskets scored for every shot taken. Express your shooting accuracy in this repetition as a percentage.

6. What is your average score per trial over the three trials?

7. How does your average in question 3 compare to your average in question 6?

8. How many baskets did you throw in total over the six trials? What is your ratio of baskets scored to shots taken? Describe this ratio in terms of baskets scored for every shot taken. Express your shooting accuracy over the six trials as a percentage.

9. What is the average number of baskets scored per trial over the six trials?

10. How does your average in question 9 compare to your averages in questions 3 and 6?

Answer Key

1. In my three five-pace trials, I scored 8 out of 10 (8/10) baskets, 7 out of 10 (7/10) baskets and 10 out of 10 (10/10) baskets.

2. In total, I scored 25 baskets over the three trials. My ratio of baskets scored to shots taken is 5:6. In other words, I scored five baskets out of every six shots. [25/30. 25/5 = 5. 30 / 5 = 6. 5:6.] In this repetition I was 83 percent accurate with my shots. [25 baskets / 30 shots x 100 = 83.3 = 83%]

3. My average score over the three trials was 8 baskets per trial. [25 baskets / 3 trials = 8.3 = 8]

4. In my three 10-pace trials, I scored 3 out of 10 (3/10) baskets, 3 out of 10 (3/10) baskets and 5 out of 10 (5/10) baskets.

5. In total, I scored 11 baskets over the three trials. My ratio of baskets scored to shots taken is 11:30. In other words, I scored 11 baskets out of every 30 shots. In this repetition I was 37 percent accurate with my shots. [11 baskets / 30 shots x 100 = 36.7 = 37%]

6. My average score over the three trials was 4 baskets per trial. [11 baskets / 3 trials = 3.7 = 4]

7. My average of eight (8) baskets in question 3 was four (4) baskets higher than my average of four (4) baskets in question 6. [8 baskets (first repetition) - 4 baskets (second repetition) = 4 baskets.]

8. In total, I threw 36 baskets over the six trials. [25 baskets (first repetition) + 11 baskets (second repetition) = 36 baskets.] My ratio of baskets scored to shots taken is 6:10 [36/60. 36 / 6 = 6. 60 / 6 = 10. 6:10] For every 10 shots taken, I scored six (6) baskets. My shooting accuracy over the six trials was 60 percent. [36 baskets scored / 60 shots taken x 100 = 60%]

9. The average number of baskets scored per trial over the six trials was six (6). [36 baskets scored / 6 trials = 6 baskets]

10. My average of six (6) baskets in question 9 is two (2) baskets lower than my average of eight (8) baskets in questions 3 [8 baskets - 6 baskets = 2 baskets] and two (2) baskets higher than my average of four (4) baskets in question 6 [6 baskets - 4 baskets = 2 baskets]

Keeping Tabs on your "T"s

Examine your T-shirt collection.

1. How many T-shirts do you own?
2. How many are dirty and awaiting a wash?
3. How many are clean and ready for wear?
4. What percentage of your T-shirt collection is clean?
5. What percentage of your T-shirt collection is dirty?
6. How many solid colored T-shirts do you own?
7. How many multicolored T-shirts do you own?
8. How many of your T-shirts are printed with a logo or a slogan?
9. Do you have more solid or multicolored T-shirts? How many more? Do you have more multicolored T-shirts or T-shirts with a logo? How many more? Do you have more T-shirts with a logo or solid colored T-shirts?
10. What percentage of your T-shirt collection is solid colored? What percentage is multicolored? What percentage has a logo or design?

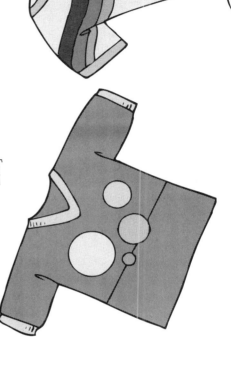

Answer Key

1. I own 65 T-shirts.
2. Seven (7) of my T-shirts are dirty and awaiting a wash.
3. Fifty-eight (58) of my T-shirts are clean and ready for wear. [65 (Ts in total) - 7 (dirty) = 58 (clean)]
4. Eighty-nine (89) percent of my T-shirts are clean. [58 (clean Ts) / 65 (Ts in total) x 100 = 89.23%]
5. Eleven (11) percent of my T-shirts are dirty. [7 (dirty Ts) / 65 (Ts in total) x 100 = 10.77%]
6. I own 39 solid colored T-shirts.
7. I own 9 multicolored T-shirts.
8. Seventeen (17) of my T-shirts are printed with a logo or a slogan. [65 (Ts in total) - 39 (solid Ts) - 9 (multi Ts) = 17.]
9. I have 30 more solid colored T-shirts than multicolored T-shirts. [39 (solid Ts) - 9 (multi Ts) = 30.] I have 8 more T-shirts with a logo than multicolored T-shirts. [17 (logo Ts) - 9 (multi Ts) = 8] I have 22 more solid colored T-shirts than T-shirts with a logo. [39 (solid Ts) - 17 (Ts with logo) = 22]
10. Sixty (60) percent of my T-shirt collection is solid colored. [39 (solid Ts) / 65 (Ts in total) x 100 = 60%] Fourteen (14) percent of my T-shirt collection is multicolored. [9 (multi Ts) / 65 (Ts in total) x 100 = 13.85 = 14%] Twenty-six (26) percent of my T-shirt collection has logos or designs. [17 (Ts with logo) / 65 (Ts in total) x 100 = 26.15 = 26%]

Activity 29

Battle of the "Blowhards"

You will need a clean tissue, a measuring tape, a smooth surface and a friend for this activity. (You might want to grab a dictionary too!)

1. Place your tissue on the blowing surface. Mark this point. In one breath, blow the tissue as far down the blowing surface as possible. How far did your tissue travel? (Take your measurement from the point of the tissue that is furthest from the start mark.)

2. Repeat the exercise four more times for a total of five blow trials.

3. List your blow trial distances in descending order. What was your furthest blow distance? What was your shortest blow distance?

4. How much further was your furthest blow distance than your shortest blow distance?

5. What was your average blow distance?

6. Have a friend or family member try this activity. List his or her five blow trial distances in ascending order.

7. What was his or her furthest blow distance? What was his or her shortest blow distance? What was the average of this "blowhard's" five blow trials?

8. Which "blowhard" had the higher blow average? What is the ratio of highest to lowest average? How much higher was this average than the lower blow average?

9. Who was the bigger single trial "blowhard"? In other words, who recorded the furthest blow distance? What was this distance and how much greater was it than the furthest blow distance recorded by the opposing "blowhard"?

10. And by the way, what is a "blowhard"? Is the champion "blowhard" really a "blowhard"?

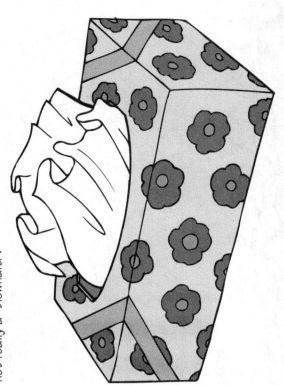

Answer Key

1. My tissue traveled 72½ inches.

2. 58 inches, 58½ inches, 68½ inches, 53 inches.

3. 7½, 68½, 58½, 58, 53. My furthest blow distance was 72½ inches. My shortest blow distance was 53 inches.

4. My furthest blow distance was 19½ inches further than my shortest blow distance. [72.5 - 53 = 19.5.]

5. My average blow distance was 62 inches. [72.5 + 58 + 58.5 + 68.5 + 53 = 310.5 inches / 5 trials = 62.1 = 62 inches.]

6. My son's blow distances: 36½, 44½, 47°, 48¾/4, 49.

7. My son's furthest blow distance was 49 inches. His shortest blow distance was 36½ inches. His average blow distance was 45 inches. [36.5 + 44.5 + 47.25 + 48.75 + 49 = 226 inches / 5 trials = 45.2 = 45 inches.]

8. I had the highest "blowhard" average. The ratio of highest to lowest average is 62:45. My average is 17 inches higher than my son's. [62 - 45 = 17.]

9. My best blow was 72½ inches, while my son's best blow was only 49 inches. I blew 23½ inches farther than my son. [72.5 - 49 = 23.5] Because I recorded the farthest single blow distance, I am the bigger single trial "blowhard".

10. A "blowhard" is one who brags, so the champion "blowhard" is not really a "blowhard".

Activity 30

Brushing Up

1. How many times do you brush your teeth in one day?
2. How many times do you brush your teeth in one week? In one month?
3. How many times do you brush your teeth in one year?
4. How long do you spend on each brushing? (Time yourself the next time your brush!)
5. How much time do you spend brushing in one day?
6. How much time do you spend brushing your teeth in one week? In one month?
7. How much time do you spend brushing your teeth in one year?
8. If there are 25 squeezes in a tube of toothpaste, how many days does a tube of toothpaste last? (Assume you are the only person using this particular tube.)
9. Assuming each member of your family brushes as frequently as you do, how long does a tube of toothpaste last your family?
10. How many tubes of toothpaste will your family use in one year?

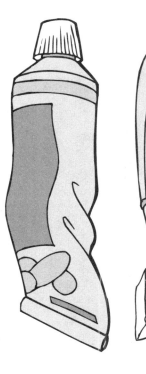

Answer Key

1. I brush my teeth three times each day.
2. In one week, I brush my teeth 21 times. [3 times/day x 7 days/week = 21] In one month, I brush my teeth 84 times. [21 times/week x 4 weeks = 84 times/month]
3. In one year, I brush my teeth 1095 times. [3 times/day x 365 days/year = 1095 times/year]
4. I spend 35 seconds on each brushing.
5. I spend 1 minute, 45 seconds (105 seconds) brushing my teeth each day. [35 seconds/brushing x 3 brushings/day = 105 seconds. 105 seconds / 60 seconds/minute = 1.75. 1 minute with 0.75 minutes remainder. 0.75 x 60 seconds/minute = 45 seconds]
6. I spend 12 minutes, 15 seconds (735 seconds) brushing my teeth in one week. [105 seconds brushing/day x 7 days/week = 735 seconds brushing/week. 735 / 60 seconds/minute = 12.25. 12 minutes with 0.25 minutes remainder. 0.25 x 60 seconds/minute = 15 seconds.] I spend 49 minutes (2940 seconds) brushing my teeth in one month. [735 seconds/week x 4 weeks/month = 2940 seconds/month. 2940 / 60 seconds/minute = 49 minutes]
7. I spend 638 minutes, 45 seconds (38,325 seconds) brushing my teeth in one year. [105 seconds/day x 365 days/year = 38,325 seconds/year. 38,325 / 60 seconds/minute = 638.75]
8. If there are 25 squeezes in a tube of toothpaste, a tube of toothpaste lasts me 8 days. [25 squeezes/tube / 3 squeezes/day = 8.3 = 8 days]
9. Assuming my family members brush their teeth as frequently as I do, a tube of toothpaste lasts us only two full days! [5 family members x 3 squeezes/day = 15 squeezes/day. 25 squeezes/tube / 15 squeezes/day = 1.6 = 2 days]
10. My family uses 219 tubes of toothpaste in one year: [15 squeezes/day x 365 days/year = 5475 squeezes/year. 5475 squeezes/year / 25 squeezes/tube = 219 tubes/year]

Challenge: How long should you brush your teeth each time to get them really clean?

Activity 31

Time Passages

Estimate how much time you spend each day:

1. Sleeping.
2. Eating.
3. At school.
4. Traveling to and from school.
5. Playing sports.
6. Doing homework.
7. Watching TV.
8. Reading and enjoying other hobbies.
9. Add up all of the time spent in questions 1 to 8. How much "spare" time remains in your day?
10. Based on your answer to question 9, how much spare time will you accumulate over the course of a year?

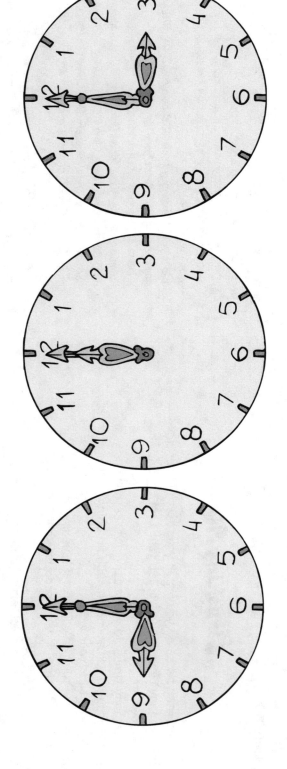

TLC10269 Copyright © Teaching & Learning Company, Carthage, IL 62321-001

ABC Hygiene

Time yourself as you sing the ABC song as a leisurely tempo. (Don't forget to add the ending, "Now I've sung my ABC's, next time won't you sing with me?")

1. How long did it take you to sing the ABC song?

2. If proper hygiene demands that you scrub for as long as it takes you to sing the alphabet song, for how long should you soap your hands before rinsing?

3. Since you must wash your hands before and after every meal, how much time each day should you spend soaping your hands? (State your answer in minutes and seconds.)

4. If you have two snacks at school, one after-school and one bedtime snack, how much more time should you spend scrubbing?

5. How much time in total, including meals and snacks, will you spend soaping each day? (State your answer in minutes and seconds.)

6. How many trips to the bathroom do you make each day?

7. Since you absolutely must wash your hands after each excursion to the toilet, how much scrubbing time do trips to the bathroom add to your day?

8. How much time do you spend washing your hands before and after meals and snacks and after trips to the toilet each day?

9. How much time do you spend washing your hands each week? (Assume that weekday and weekend washing habits are the same. State your answer in minutes and seconds.)

10. How much time do you spend washing your hands each year? (State your answer in hours and minutes.)

Answer Key

1. It took me 24 seconds to sing the ABC song.

2. If proper hygiene demands that I scrub for as long as it takes me to sing the alphabet song, I should soap my hands for 24 seconds before rinsing.

3. Since I must wash my hands before and after every meal, I should spend two (2) minutes, 24 seconds (2:24) soaping my hands each day. [24 seconds/soaping × 3 meals × 2 (before/after) = 144 seconds. 144 seconds / 60 seconds/minute = 2.4. 2 minutes with 0.4 minutes remainder. 0.4 × 60 seconds/minute = 24 seconds. 2 minutes, 24 seconds]

4. If I have two snacks at school, one after-school and one bedtime snack, I should spend 192 more seconds scrubbing. [24 seconds/soaping × 4 snacks × 2 (before/after) = 192 seconds]

5. In total, I will spend five (5) minutes, 36 seconds (5:36) soaping each day. [144 seconds (meals) + 192 seconds (snacks) = 336 seconds. 336 seconds / 60 seconds/minute = 5.6. 5 minutes with 0.6 minutes remainder. 0.6 minutes remainder × 60 seconds/minute = 36 seconds remainder. 0.6 minutes remainder. 5 minutes, 36 seconds]

6. I make five (5) trips to the bathroom each day.

7. Since I absolutely must wash my hands after each excursion to the toilet, bathroom trips add 120 seconds scrubbing time to my day. [24 seconds/soaping × 5 bathroom trips = 120 seconds]

8. I spend seven (7) minutes, 36 seconds (7:36) washing my hands before and after meals and snacks and after trips to the toilet each day. [144 (meals) + 192 (snacks) + 120 (bathroom trips) = 456 seconds. 456 seconds / 60 seconds/minute = 7.6. 7 minutes with 0.6 minutes remainder. 0.6 seconds remainder × 60 seconds/minute = 36 seconds remainder. 0.6 seconds remainder × 60 seconds/minute = 36 seconds, 7 minutes, 36 seconds]

9. I spend 53 minutes, 12 seconds (53:12) washing my hands each week. [456 seconds/day × 7 days/week = 3192 seconds/week. 3192 seconds/day × 7 days/week = 3192 seconds/week. 3192 seconds / 60 seconds/hour = 53.2 minutes. 53 minutes with 0.2 minutes remainder. 0.2 minutes remainder × 60 seconds/minute = 12 seconds. 53 minutes, 12 seconds]

10. I spend 46 hours, 7 minutes washing my hands each year. [3192 seconds/week × 52 weeks/year = 165,984 seconds/year. 165,984 seconds/year / 60 seconds/minute = 2,766.4. 2,766.4 / 60 minutes/hour = 46.11 hours. 46 hours with 0.11 hours remainder. 0.11 hours remainder × 60 minutes/hour = 6.6 = 7 minutes. 46 hours, 7 minutes]

Activity 33

Bath Time

1. Next time you take a shower or a bath, time how long you spend in the tub. Record this time.

2. If everyone in your household takes the same amount of time to shower or bathe as you do, for how much time will the tub be in use on bath day?

3. If the kids in your household spend twice as long in the shower as the adults, how much tub time will your family log on bath day?

4. Assuming you bathe or shower for the same amount of time every day, how much tub time do you spend in the shower each week?

5. If you use five-and-one-half (5.5) gallons of water each time you get into the tub or shower, how much water will you use in one week?

6. If you bathe or shower twice as often, how much time will you spend in the tub each month? How many gallons of water will you use?

7. What if you cut your bathing/showering time in half? How much time will you spend in the tub over the course of the next year? How much water will you use?

8. If everyone in your family bathes or showers three times each week, how much time will your family spend in the tub over the next 1/2 year?

9. Based on the information in questions 5 and 8, how much water will your family use over the next year?

10. Let's say your bathing/showering time decreases by 10 seconds every year, starting this year. How much time will you spend in the shower when I am 50?

Answer Key

1. My last shower took 13 minutes.

2. If everyone in my household takes the same amount of time to shower or bathe as I do, the tub will be in use for 65 minutes, or one hour, five minutes (1:05) on each bath day. [13 minutes/person x 5 people = 65 minutes]

3. If the kids in my household spend twice as long in the shower as the adults, my family will log 104 minutes, or one (1) hour, 44 minutes (1:44) of tub time on bath day. [13 minutes x 3 kids x 2 = 78 minutes. 78 minutes x 2 adults = 26 minutes. 78 minutes (kids) + 26 minutes (adults) = 104 minutes.] [To transfigure minutes into hours: 104 minutes / 60 minutes/hour = 1.73. 1 hour with 0.73 hours remainder. 0.73 hours remainder x 60 minutes/hour = 43.8 = 44 minutes. 1 hour, 44 minutes.

4. Assuming I shower for the same amount of time every day, I spend 52 minutes in the shower each week. [13 minutes/shower x 4 showers/week = 52 minutes]

5. If I use five-and-one-half (5.5) gallons of water each time I get into the shower, I will use 22 gallons of water in one week. [5.5 gallons/shower x 4 showers/week = 22 gallons]

6. If I shower twice as often, I will spend 416 minutes or 4 hours, 56 minutes (4:56) in the shower each month [13 minutes/shower x 4 showers/week x 2 x 4 weeks/month = 416 minutes] and I will use 176 gallons of water. [5.5 gallons/shower x 4 showers/week x 2 x 4 weeks/month =176 gallons]

7. If I cut my shower time in half, I will spend 1,352 minutes or 22 hours, 32 minutes (22:32) in the shower over the course of the next year. [13 minutes/shower / 2 = 6.5 minutes/shower. 6.5 minutes/shower x 4 showers/week x 52 weeks/year = 1352 minutes] and I will use 572 gallons of water. [5.5 gallons/shower / 2 = 2.75 gallons/shower. 2.75 gallons/shower x 4 showers/week x 52 weeks/year = 572 gallons]

8. If everyone in my family showers three times each week, we will spend 5070 minutes or 84 hours, 30 minutes (84:30) in the tub over the next 1/2 year. [13 minutes/shower x 5 family members x 3 showers/week x 26 weeks (52 weeks/year / 2 = 26) = 5070 minutes.]

9. Based on the information in questions 5 and 8, my family will use 4290 gallons of water over the next year. [5.5 gallons/shower x 5 family members x 3 showers/week x 52 weeks = 4290]

10. If my shower time decreases by 10 seconds every year, starting this year, I will spend 10 minutes, 50 seconds (or 650 seconds) in the shower when I am 50? [50 years (projected age) - 37 years (current age) = 13 years. 13 years x 10 seconds/year = 130 seconds. 13 minutes (current shower time) x 60 seconds/minute = 780 seconds. 780 seconds (current shower time) - 130 seconds (time decrease) = 650 seconds. 650 seconds / 60 second/minute = 10.83. 10 minutes with 0.83 minutes remainder. 0.83 x 60 seconds/minute = 49.8 = 50 seconds. 10 minutes, 50 seconds.]

TLC10269 Copyright © Teaching & Learning Company, Carthage, IL 62321-001

Activity 34

Transcription Test

For this activity, you will a piece of paper and a pen or pencil, a computer or typewriter with paper, some text from which to copy, and a watch or timer.

1. Time yourself for one minute. Copying from the text in front of you, how many words can you (accurately) print, write or type in this time?

2. Try a different block of text and time yourself for another minute. How many words did you print, write or type this time?

3. One more time! A new block of text and one more minute. How many words did you print, write or type this time?

4. Averaging your three times together, how many words can you print, write or type in one minute?

5. Based on your highest word score, how many words could you print, write or type in five (5) minutes?

6. Based on your lowest word score, how many words could you print, write or type in (5) minutes?

7. How many more words could you transcribe in question 5 than in question 6?

8. Based on your average in question 4, how many words could you print, write or type in 10 minutes?

9. Based on your average in question 4, how many words could you print, write or type in ½ hour?

10. Based on your average in question 4, how many words could you print, write or type in 1 hour? Do you think this estimate is accurate? Why or why not?

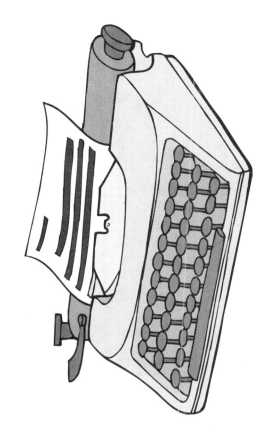

Answer Key

1. In the first trial, I typed 92 words in one minute.

2. In the second trial, I typed 79 words in one minute.

3. In the third trial, I typed 88 words in one minute.

4. On average, I can type 86 words per minute. [92 words (1st trial) + 79 words (2nd trial) + 88 words (3rd trial) = 259 words total. 259 words total / 3 trials = 86.33 = 86 words]

5. Based on my highest word score, I could type 460 words in five (5) minutes. [92 words/minute x 5 minutes = 460 words.]

6. Based on my lowest word score, I could type 395 words in (5) minutes. [79 words/minute x 5 minutes = 395 words]

7. I could transcribe 65 more words in question 5 than in question 6. [460 words (question 5) - 395 words (question 6) = 65 words.]

8. Based on my average in question 4, I could type 860 words in 10 minutes. [86 words/minute x 10 minutes = 860 words.]

9. Based on my average in question 4, I could type 2580 words in ½ hour. [86 words/minute x 30 minutes = 2580 words.]

10. Based on my average in question 4, I could type 5160 words in one (1) hour. [86 words/minute x 60 minutes = 5160 words]

Video Viewers

1. What is the running time of your favorite TV home video? (If you don't have any videos at home, ask a friend or relative to provide you with the data for this activity.)

2. How many movie previews precede the movie?

3. How much time do the movie previews take?

4. For what percentage of the running time of the movie do the previews account?

5. What is the average length of a movie preview?

6. How long are the opening credits? For what percentage of the running time of the movie do the opening credits account?

7. How long are the closing credits? For what percentage of the running time of the movie do the closing credits account?

8. For what percentage of the running time of the movie do the previews and the opening and closing credits account?

9. For what percentage of the running time of the movie does the feature presentation account?

10. Excluding previews and opening and closing credits, how long is the movie?

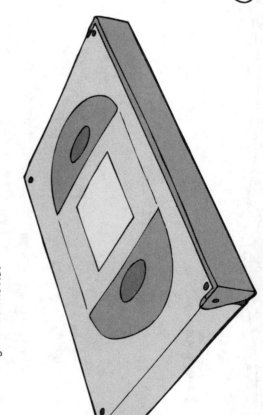

Answer Key

1. The running time of my daughter's favorite TV home video is 74 minutes.

2. Five movie previews precede the movie.

3. The movie previews take 5 minutes and 30 seconds (or 330 seconds). [5 minutes x 60 seconds/minute = 300 seconds + 30 seconds = 330 seconds]

4. The previews account for seven (7) percent of the running time of the movie. [74 minutes x 60 seconds/minute = 4440 seconds. 330 seconds (previews) / 4440 seconds (total running time of movie) x 100 = 7.4 = 7%]

5. The average length of a movie preview is 66 seconds. [330 seconds / 5 previews = 66 seconds/preview]

6. The opening credits are four (4) minutes long. The opening credits account for five (5) percent of the running time of the movie. [4 minutes x 60 seconds/minute = 240 seconds. 240 seconds (opening credits) / 4440 seconds (total running time of movie) x 100 = 5.4 = 5%]

7. The closing credits are four (4) minutes long. The closing credits account for five (5) percent of the running time of the movie. [4 minutes x 60 seconds/minute = 240 seconds. 240 seconds (opening credits) / 4440 seconds (total running time of movie) x 100 = 5.4 = 5%]

8. The previews and the opening and closing credits account for 17% of the running time of the movie. [7% + 5% + 5% = 17%.]

9. The feature presentation accounts for 83 percent of the running time of the movie. [100% - 17% = 83%.]

10. Excluding previews and opening and closing credits, the movie is 60 minutes, 30 seconds (or 3630 seconds) long. [330 seconds + 240 seconds + 240 seconds = 810 seconds (total running time) - 810 seconds (previews, opening/closing credits) = 3630 seconds. 3630 seconds / 60 seconds/minute = 60.5 minutes. 60 minutes with 0.5 minutes remainder. 0.5 (minutes remainder) x 60 seconds/minute = 30 seconds. 60 minutes, 30 seconds]

Eat and Sleep

1. What time did you go to bed last night?
2. What time did you get up this morning?
3. How much sleep did you get?
4. How long have you been awake?
5. What time are you planning to go to bed tonight? How many hours will you have been awake if you go to bed at that time?
6. If you go to bed at 9:45 p.m., how many hours will it have been since you last went to bed?
7. If you skipped breakfast and ate lunch at 12:30 p.m., how long would you have to wait between waking and eating?
8. If you had a small snack for breakfast and lunch, but did not eat a full meal until dinner at 6:15 p.m., how long would you have to wait between waking and eating a full meal?
9. If you go to bed according to your prediction in question 5, how long will you have to digest your dinner if you finish your meal at 6:30 p.m.?
10. How long did you go without food if you ate a bedtime snack at 8:30 p.m. last night and breakfast as soon as you woke up this morning?

Answer Key

1. I went to bed at 10:30 p.m. last night.
2. I got up at 6:45 a.m. this morning.
3. I got 8 hours and 15 minutes sleep, or 495 [8 (hours) x 60 (minutes/hour) = 480 (minutes) + 15 (additional minutes) = 495 minutes.]
4. It is now 7:47 p.m. I have been awake for 13 hours and two (2) minutes or 782 minutes. [13 (hours) x 60 (hours/minute) = 780 (minutes) + 2 (additional minutes) = 782 minutes.]
5. I am planning to go to bed at 11:00 tonight. I will have been awake for 16 hours and 15 minutes or 975 minutes. [16 (hours) x 60 (minutes/hour) = 960. 960 + 15 = 975 minutes.]
6. If I go to bed at 9:45 p.m., it will have been 23 hours and 15 minutes, 1395 minutes, since I last went to bed. [23 (hours) x 60 (minutes/hour) = 1380 + 15 = 1395.]
7. If I skipped breakfast and ate lunch at 12:30 p.m., I would have to wait for 5 hours and 15 minutes between waking and eating.
8. If I did not eat a full meal until dinner at 6:15 p.m., I would have to wait for 11 1/2 hours between waking and eating a full meal.
9. If I finish dinner at 6:30 p.m. and go to bed at 11:00 p.m. (as I planned in question 5), I will have 4 1/2 hours.
10. If I ate a bedtime snack at 8:30 p.m. last night and breakfast as soon as I woke up this morning, I went 10 hours and 15 minutes without food.

Color by Number

1. Draw a picture. (Make it fairly detailed.) Make two photocopies of your picture.

2. Color the original picture, using different colored pencils, crayons or markers. Assign each of the colors a different number.

3. On one photocopy, use your completed picture from question 2 as a guide to write numbers in the spaces where numbers should be. (Make sure every enclosed space is assigned a color.) Write/draw the color key at the bottom of your picture.

4. Write the same numbers on the other photocopy as you did on the photocopy in question 3. This time, however, change the color key at the bottom of the page. (Switch the colors and the numbers so that no color/number correspondents are repeated from question 3.)

5. Ask a friend to color the photocopy in question 3. Do the two pictures look identical? Color the photocopy in question 4 yourself. Does this picture look like your picture in question 2?

6. Add all of the numbers in your picture in question 4 together. What is the sum?

7. Multiply the sum in question 6 by the number of numbers used in your picture. What is the product?

8. Express the product in question 7 in words.

9. Assign a place value to each digit in the product in question 7.

10. Reverse the digits in the number in question 7. What is the new number in words? Assign a place value to each digit in the new number.

1. Light Brown
2. Dark Brown
3. Black
4. Cream

Answer Key

1. Draw a picture and make two photocopies. See example of the dog below.
2. 1. Light Brown, 2. Dark Brown, 3. Black, 4. Cream.
3. See picture below.
4. 1. Cream, 2. Black, 3. Dark Brown, 4. Light Brown.
5. Answers will vary.
6. The sum of the numbers used in my picture is 21. [1 + 1 + 1 + 1 + 1 + 1 + 1 + 1 + 2 + 3 + 4 + 4=21]
7. Multiplying the product in question 6 by the number of numbers used in my picture yields a product of 84. [21 product × 4 number of numbers = 84.]
8. Expressed in words, 84 is eighty four.
9. Assigning place value to 84: 8 tens, 4 ones.
10. If I reverse the digits in the number in question 7 - 84 - I get a new number of 48. In words, the new number is forty eight. Assigning a place value to 48: 4 tens, 8 ones.

Activity 38

Bookworms

In this activity, you will take an inventory of the books in your bedroom and home. If you would rather do this activity at school, substitute the books in your classroom and school library for those in your bedroom and home. (You'll need to ask the school librarian to provide you with some data if you go this route.) If you are having trouble gathering data, use your imagination and create a couple of really neat book collections, one for you and one for your entire household!

1. How many books do you have in your bedroom, classroom or imaginary collection?

2. How many of the book have soft covers? How many have hard covers?

3. Do more of the books have soft or hard covers? How many more?

4. What percent of the books have soft covers?

5. What percent of the books have hard covers?

6. How many of the books have you never read? What percent of the books have you never read?

7. How many of the books have you read more than once? What percent of the books have you read more than once? How many of the books have you read three time or more? What percent of the books have you read at least three times?

8. How many books are in your household, school library or imaginary collection? (If there are too many books in your household to count in a few minutes, estimate. If you are using the school library collection, ask your librarian. If you are using your imagination, well, go for it!)

9. How many more books are there in your household, school library or imaginary household collection are in your bedroom, classroom or imaginary bedroom collection?

10. What percent of the total number of books in your household, school library or imaginary household collection are in your bedroom, classroom or imaginary bedroom collection?

Answer Key

1. I have 114 books in my bedroom.

2. Eighty (80) of the books in my bedroom have soft covers. Thirty-four (34) of the books in my bedroom have hard covers.

3. I have 46 more softcover books than hardcover books in my bedroom.

4. Seventy (70) percent of the books in my bedroom have soft covers. [80 soft books / 114 books total × 100 = 70.2 = 70%]

5. Thirty (30) percent of the books in my bedroom have hard covers. [34 hard books / 114 books total × 100 = 29.8 = 30%]

6. There are 16 books in my room that I have never read. I have yet to read 14 percent of the books in my room. [16 books (never read) / 114 books (total) × 100 = 14.1 = 14%]

7. There are 18 books in my room that I have read more than once. I have read 16 percent of the books in my room more than once. [18 books (more than once) / 114 books (total) × 100 = 15.8 = 16%. There are six (6) books in my room that I have read more than three times. I have read five (5) percent of my books at least three times. [6 books (at least three times) / 114 books (total) × 100 = 5.3 = 5%]

8. My family possesses approximately 1100 books.

9. There are 986 more books in my household than there are in my room. [1100 books (total) - 114 books (my room) = 986 books]

10. Ten (10) percent of the total number of books in my household are in my room. [114 books (my room) × 1100 books (total) × 100 = 10.4 = 10%]

Musical Measurements

Study the song times on your favorite CD or cassette.

1. What is the length of the longest song on the CD?
2. What is the length of the shortest song?
3. Put the songs in order according to their length, starting with the shortest.
4. How long is your favorite song? According to song length, how does it rank?
5. Add all of the song times together. What is the total running time of your CD?
6. What is the average length of the songs on the CD?
7. What percentage of the total running time does your favorite song account for?
8. How long would your favorite song run if it were twice as long?
9. If you took away the two longest songs, what would be the running time of your CD? What if you took away the two shortest songs?
10. Choose the four songs that you like the least. Subtract their times from the CD. How much time would need to be filled? Approximately how many times could your favorite song be repeated to fill this time?

Answer Key

1. The longest song is (five) 5 minutes and 31 seconds, or 331 seconds. [5 (minutes) x 60 (seconds/minute) = 300 seconds + 31 seconds = 331 seconds]
2. The shortest song is (two) 2 minutes 46 seconds, or 166 seconds.
3. 2:46; 3:05; 3:22; 4:00; 4:09; 4:10; 4:18; 4:38; 5:08; 5:31.
4. My favorite song is (four) 4 minutes and 38 seconds long. It is the third longest song.

5. The total running time of my CD is 45 minutes and 25 seconds or 2725 seconds. [2:46 (166 seconds) + 3:05 (185) + 3:22 (202) + 4:00 (240) + 4:09 (249) + 4:10 (250) + 4:18 (258) + 4:18 (258) + 4:38 (278) + 5:08 (308) + 5:31 (331) = 2725 seconds. 2725 (total seconds) / 60 (seconds/minute) = 45.42 minutes. 0.42 minutes (remainder) x 60 (seconds/minute) = 25.2 = 25 seconds. 45 minutes, 25 seconds]

6. The average length of a song on my CD is 4 minutes and 8 seconds or 248 seconds long. [2725 seconds (total) / 11 songs (on CD) = 247.7 = 248. 248 seconds / 60 seconds/minute = 4.13 minutes. 0.13 minutes (remainder) x 60 = 7.8 = 8 seconds. 4 minutes, 8 seconds]

7. My favorite song accounts for 10 percent of the total running time of the CD. [278 seconds (favorite song) / 2725 seconds (total songs) x 100 = 10.2 = 10%]

8. If my favorite song were twice as long, it would run for 556 seconds, or nine (9) minutes, 16 seconds. [278 + 278 = 556 seconds. 556 seconds / 60 seconds/minute = 9.27 minutes. 0.27 minutes (remainder) x 60 (seconds/minute) = 16.2 = 16 seconds. 9 minutes, 16 seconds]

9. If I took away the two longest songs, the running time of my CD would be 2086 seconds or 34 minutes and 46 seconds. [2725 - 331 - 308 = 2086. 2086 seconds / 60 (seconds/minute) = 34.77 minutes. 0.77 minutes (remainder) x 60 seconds/minute = 46.2 = 46 seconds. 34 minutes, 46 seconds.] If I took away the two shortest songs, the running time of my CD would be 2374 or 39 minutes, 34 seconds. [2725 - 166 - 185 = 2374. 2374 seconds / 60 seconds/minute = 39.57 minutes. 0.57 minutes (remainder) = 34.2 = 34 seconds. 39 minutes, 34 seconds]

10. If I subtracted the times of the four songs I like the least from my CD, I would need to fill 983 seconds. [250 + 308 + 240 + 185 = 983.] I could repeat my favorite song approximately 3½ times in this time. [983 seconds (to be filled) / 278 seconds (favorite song) = 3.54 = 3.5]

Balloon Smack

Ask a parent if you can blow up a balloon for use in this activity. You will also need a measuring tape, a piece of string, a penny, a piece of paper, a pencil or pen, and a friend.

1. Mark a start line with the piece of string. Stand with your toes behind the start line. Smack the balloon as far as you can. Have your friend mark the spot where the balloon touches the ground with the penny. Measure the distance from the start line to the penny. How far did you smack the balloon? Record your distance on the piece of paper. Smack the balloon twice more and record your distances.

2. Switch places with your friend. Have your friend smack the balloon three times while you record his or her distances.

3. What was the total distance of your three smacks?

4. What is the mean distance of your three smacks? What was the median (middle) distance of your three smacks? What is the difference between your mean and median smack distances?

5. How much further than your shortest smack was your furthest smack?

6. For what percentage of your total smack distance does your furthest smack account?

7. What was the total distance of your friend's three smacks?

8. What was the mean distance of your friend's three smacks? What was the median (middle) distance of your friend's three smacks? What is the difference between your friend's mean and median smack distances?

9. Who had the furthest average smack distance? How much further was this than the other person's average smack distance?

10. Who had the longest single smack? How much further was this smack than the other person's furthest smack? Who had the shortest single smack? How much shorter was this smack than the other person's shortest smack?

Answer Key

1. I smacked the balloon 125.5 inches, 119 inches and 137.5 inches. My son, Matthew, smacked the balloon 136.5 inches, 141.5 inches and 124.5 inches.

2. The total distance of my three smacks was 382 inches. [125.5 + 119 + 137.5 = 382]

3. The mean distance of my three smacks was 127 inches. [382 total smacks / 3 trials = 127.3 = 127.] The median (middle) distance of my three smacks was 125.5. [137.5, 125.5, 119.] The difference between my mean smack and my median smack is 1.5 inches. [127 inches (mean) - 125.5 inches (median) = 1.5 inches]

4. My furthest smack was 18.5 inches further than my shortest smack. [137.5 - 119 = 18.5]

5. My furthest smack accounts for 40 percent of my total smack distance. [137.5 furthest smack / 382 total smack distance x 100 = 35.9 = 40%]

6. The total distance of Matthew's three smacks was 402.5 inches. [136.5 + 141.5 + 124.5 = 402.5]

7. The mean distance of Matthew's three smacks was 134 inches. [402.5 total smacks / 3 trials = 134.2 = 134.] The median (middle) distance of Matthew's three smacks was 136.5 inches. [141.5, 136.5, 124.5.] The difference between Matthew's median smack and his mean smack is 2.5 inches. [136.5 inches (median) - 134 inches (mean) = 2.5 inches]

8. Matthew had the furthest average smack distance. His average smack distance of 134 inches was seven (7) inches further than my average smack distance of 127 inches. [134 inches (Matthew's average) - 127 inches (my average) = 7 inches]

9. Matthew had the longest single smack. His longest smack of 141.5 inches was four (4) inches longer than my longest smack of 137.5 inches. [141.5 inches (Matthew's longest smack) - 137.5 inches (my longest smack) = 4 inches.] I had the shortest single smack. My shortest smack of 119 inches was 5.5 inches shorter than Matthew's shortest smack of 124.5 inches. [124.5 inches (Matthew's shortest smack) - 119 inches (my shortest smack) = 5.5 inches]

Activity 41

Stepping Out

1. Count and record the number of steps from your bed to the front door.

2. Count and record the number of steps from your bed to the sink in the nearest bathroom.

3. Count and record the number of steps from your bed to your place at the kitchen table.

4. Count and record the number of steps from your bed to the chair or couch nearest the television or computer.

5. Count and record the number of steps from your bed to the nearest telephone.

6. If you needed a drink of water in the middle of the night, how many steps would you take getting to the sink and back to bed again?

7. If you went in the front door from school and went straight to your bedroom to read, then went out to eat dinner and retired to your bed for the evening straight from the table, how many steps would you travel?

8. If you had to answer the telephone three (3) times in one night, how many steps would you travel?

9. If you got up on Saturday morning, gave your face a quick wash, returned to your bedroom to make your bed, went out and turned on the television, returned to your bedside to change out of your pajamas, and sat down at the kitchen table for breakfast, how many steps would you travel?

10. If you jumped up in the middle of the night to answer the phone (wrong number!) and went back to bed; got up to quench a sudden thirst and went back to bed; let the cat in the front door and went back to bed; and then watched a little television to make myself sleepy before going to bed for good, how many steps would you travel on your nocturnal wanderings?

Answer Key

1. There are 20 steps between my bed and the front door.

2. There are eight (8) steps from my bed to the nearest sink.

3. There are 28 steps from my bed to my place at the kitchen table.

4. There are 27 steps from my bed to the couch nearest the TV.

5. There are 35 steps from my bed to the nearest telephone.

6. If I needed a drink of water in the middle of the night, I would take 16 steps getting to the sink and back to bed again. [8 steps (to the sink from bed) + 8 steps (from the sink to bed) = 16 steps]

7. If I went in the front door from school and went straight to my bed to read, then went out to eat dinner and retired to my bed for the evening straight from the table, I would travel 76 steps. [20 steps (from front door to bed) + 28 steps (from bed to kitchen table) + 28 steps (from kitchen table to bed) = 76 steps]

8. If I had to answer the telephone three (3) times in one night, I would travel 140 steps. [35 steps (from bed to the telephone) + 35 steps (from the telephone to bed) x 3 (trips) = 140 steps]

9. If I got up on Saturday morning, gave my face a quick wash, returned to my bedroom to make my bed, went out and turned on the television, returned to my bedside to change out of my pajamas, and sat down at the kitchen table for breakfast I would travel 98 steps. [8 steps (from bed to sink) + 8 steps (from sink to bed) + 27 steps (from bed to TV) + 27 steps (from TV to bed) + 28 steps (to kitchen table) = 98]

10. If I jumped up in the middle of the night to answer the phone (wrong number!) and went back to bed; got up to quench a sudden thirst and went back to bed; let the cat in the front door and went back to bed; and got up to watch a little television to make myself sleepy before going to bed for good, I would travel 180 steps on my nocturnal wanderings. [35 steps (from bed to phone) + 35 steps (from phone to bed) + 8 steps (from bed to sink) + 8 steps (from sink to bed) + 20 steps (from bed to door) + 20 steps (from door to bed) + 27 steps (from bed to TV) + 27 steps (from TV to bed) = 180 steps]

Activity 42

Television Times

Watch your favorite ½ hour television program. (You will need a scratch pad, pencil and a digital watch — or analogue watch with a second hand — for this activity.)

1. At what time did your program actually start? (Do not count musical openings and credits.)

2. At what time did your program actually end? (Do not count musical closings and credits.)

3. How long did the (musical) openings and closings last?

4. How many commercial breaks did you count in the 30 minutes?

5. How many individual commercials were aired during the 30 minutes?

6. How long was each commercial break?

7. How many seconds was the running time of the average commercial?

8. How much of the program's 30-minute running time was dedicated to advertisements (including station promotion)?

9. How much actual show time was offered in that 30-minute time slot?

10. If you watched the same program every day for one week, how much of the actual show—minus commercials and station promotion—would you see? If you watched the same program once a week for one year, how much of the actual show would you see?

Answer Key

1. My program started at 7:02.

2. My program ended at 7:26.

3. The musical openings and closings lasted for one (1) minute.

4. There were three (3) commercial breaks in the 30 minutes.

5. Twenty-five (25) commercials aired during the 30 minutes.

6. Each commercial break was three (3) minutes or 180 seconds long. [3 minutes x 60 seconds/minute = 180 seconds]

7. The running time of the average commercial was 22 seconds. [180 seconds/break x 3 breaks = 540. 540 commercial seconds / 25 commercials = 21.6 = 22 seconds]

8. Nine (9) minutes of the program's 30-minute running time were dedicated to advertisements (including station promotion). [3 minutes/break x 3 breaks = 9 minutes]

9. Twenty (20) minutes of actual show time were offered in the 30-minute time slot. [1 minute (opening and closing) + 9 minutes (commercials/station promotion) = 10. 30 minutes - 10 minutes = 20 minutes]

10. If I watched the same program every day for one week, I would see 2 hours, 18 minutes (or 140 minutes) of the actual show. [20 minutes/day x 7 days/week = 140 minutes. 140 / 60 minute/hour = 2.3. 2 hours with 0.3 hours remainder. 0.3 x 60 minute/hour = 18 minutes. 2 hours, 18 minutes.] If I watched the same program once a week for one year, I would see 17 hours, 18 minutes (or 1040 minutes) of the actual show. [20 minutes/week x 52 weeks/year = 1040 minutes/year: 1040 / 60 minutes/hour = 17.3. 17 hours with 0.3 hours remainder: 17 hours, 18 minutes]

TLC10269 Copyright © Teaching & Learning Company, Carthage, IL 62321-0010

Activity 43

The Seconds-Count Scavenger Hunt

Since this scavenger hunt is more about collecting time than it is about gathering objects, you will have to ask someone in your household to time you during your quest. The timer's job is to record the time it takes you to retrieve each object on the list. To start, stand at your front door. At the timer's signal, set off to find the first item on the list. Take this item back to the front door. Write your round-trip time for Item 1 on a sheet of paper.
Repeat these steps for Items 2 through 10.
(You must retrieve the items in order from 1 to 10.)

The Seconds-Count Scavenger Hunt Items List

Item #1:   a tissue
Item #2:   a broom or vacuum cleaner attachment
Item #3:   a piece of bread or a cookie
Item #4:   a book or magazine
Item #5:   a stuffed toy
Item #6:   a hat
Item #7:   a photograph
Item #8:   a spoon
Item #9:   a toothbrush
Item #10:   something that starts with the letter p

1. How long did it take you to complete the Seconds-Count Scavenger Hunt?
2. List your round trip times for each of the 10 items.
3. Which item was the easiest to find and retrieve? What was your round trip time for this item?
4. Which item was the most difficult to find and retrieve? What was your round trip time for this item?
5. How much longer was your slowest round trip than your quickest round trip?
6. How long was your average round trip?
7. Which trip time was closest to your trip average?
8. If you could eliminate your slowest and quickest round trips, how long would your total trip have taken? How would this affect your trip average?
9. What was your median trip time?
10. If you doubled the time of each trip, what would be your trip total? If you halved the time of each trip, what would be your trip total?

Answer Key

1. It took me 131 seconds (or two minutes, 11 seconds) to complete the Seconds-Count Scavenger Hunt.
2. A tissue–12 seconds; a broom or vacuum cleaner attachment–5 seconds; a piece of bread or a cookie–23 seconds; a book or magazine–4 seconds; a stuffed toy–14 seconds; a hat–5 seconds; a photo-graph–10 seconds; a spoon–16 seconds; a toothbrush–12 seconds; something that starts with the letter p–30 seconds.
3. The book or magazine was the easiest item to find and retrieve. My round-trip time for this item was four (4) seconds.
4. The letter p item was the most difficult to find and retrieve. My round trip time for this item was 30 seconds.
5. My slowest round trip was 26 seconds slower than my quickest round trip. [30 seconds – 4 seconds = 26 seconds]
6. My average round trip was 13.1 seconds. [131 seconds (total trip) / 10 trips = 13.1 seconds]
7. At 14 seconds, my "stuffed toy" trip was closest to my trip average of 13.1 seconds. [14 seconds (closest over trip) - 13.1 seconds (trip average) = 0.9 seconds. 13.1 seconds (trip average) - 12 seconds (closest under trip) = 1.1 second]
8. If I could eliminate my slowest and quickest round trips, my total trip would have taken [131 seconds (total trip) - 30 seconds (slowest trip) - 4 seconds (quickest trip) = 97 seconds.] This would decrease my trip average by one second to 12.1 seconds. [97 seconds (total trip) / 8 (trips) =12.125 = 12.1 seconds]
9. My median trip time was 12 seconds. [30, 23, 16, 14, 12, 12, 10, 5, 5, 4. 12 (first middle number) + 12 (second middle number) = 24 / 2 = 12]
10. If I doubled the time of each trip, my trip total would be 262 seconds or four (4) minutes, 22 seconds. [131 x 2 = 262. OR: 262 (seconds) / 60 (seconds/minute) = 4.36. .36 (remainder) x 60 (seconds/minute) = 21.6 = 22 seconds. 4 minutes, 22 seconds.] If I halved the time of each trip, my trip total would be 65.5 seconds or one (1) minute, 5½ seconds. [131 / 2 = 65.5 seconds. 65.5 seconds / 60 seconds/minute = 1.0916. .0916 (remainder) x 60 (seconds/minute) = 5.5 seconds. 1 minute, 5.5 seconds]

Activity 44

Ad Adding

Pick up a magazine published within the last six (6) months. Look at every page (including front and back covers) and count the advertisements that you see. (You might want to keep a running tally for this activity. On a piece of paper write the headings: ads; ads that direct readers to a www site; ads that are devoted entirely to promoting a www site. An ad that is selling a www site will have the stroke in all three columns because it is an ad, it directs readers to a www site and it is devoted to "selling" a www site. An ad that makes mention of a www site will have a stroke in the first two columns—it is an ad and it directs readers to a www site. All other ads will have a stroke only in the first column.)

1. How many advertisements appear in the magazine?
2. How many ads direct readers to www (world wide web) sites for more information?
3. How many ads are designed expressly to "sell" a web site?
4. How many ads make no reference to a web site?
5. What percentage of the ads direct readers to a web site?
6. What percentage of the ads are designed to "sell" a web site?
7. What percentage of the ads make no reference to a web site?
8. What kind of ad is more popular in the magazine, those that make mention of a web site or those that do not? How much more popular?
9. What percent of all ads that make mention of a web site are designed expressly to "sell" that web site?
10. Try to look at a magazine that was published more than one year ago. Has the ad ratio—in terms of ads that make reference to a web site and ads that do not—changed dramatically? What about a magazine that was published five years ago?

Answer Key

1. There are 95 advertisements in the magazine.
2. Sixty-two (62) ads direct readers to www sites for more information.
3. Ten (10) ads are designed expressly to "sell" a web site.
4. Thirty-three (33) ads make no reference to a web site. [95 - 62 = 33]
5. Sixty-five (65) percent of the ads direct readers to a web site. [62 ads (with www) / 95 ads (total) x 100 = 65.3 = 65%]
6. Ten (10) percent of the ads are designed to "sell" a web site. [10 ads ("sell" www) / 95 ads (total) x 100 = 10.5 = 10%]
7. Thirty-five (35) percent of the ads make no reference to a web site. [33 ads (conventional) / 95 ads (total) x100 = 34.7 = 35%]
8. Ads that make mention of a web site are more popular in the magazine than those that do not. There are 29 more ads that mention a web site than ads that do not. [62 - 33 = 29]
9. Sixteen (16) percent of ads that refer readers to a web site are designed expressly to "sell" that web site. [10 ads ("selling" www) / 62 ads (with www) x 100 = 16.1 = 16%]

A(d) Matter of Size

Pick up a magazine published within the last six (6) months. Look at every page (including front and back covers) and count the advertisements that you see. (You might want to keep a running tally for this activity. On a piece of paper write the headings: Full page; 1/2 page; 1/3 page; 2/3 page; 1/4 page; Multi-page spreads. Make sure to write the number of pages of each ad in the multi-page spread column.)

1. How many advertisements appear in the magazine?
2. How many ads of each size appear in the magazine?
3. What percentage of the ads are full-page ads?
4. What percentage of the ads are 1/2-page ads?
5. What percentage of the ads are 1/3-page or 2/3-page ads?
6. What percentage of the ads are 1/4-page ads?
7. What percentage of the ads are multi-page spreads? For what percentage of the total number of ad pages do these ads account?
8. How many pages in length is the magazine (including front and back covers)? For what percentage of the magazine's pages do full-page ads account? (Make sure you include the multi-page spreads.)
9. Add together the 1/2-page, 1/3-page, 2/3-page and 1/4-page ads. How many full pages do these ads represent?
10. For what percentage of the magazine's total pages do ads account? How much of the magazine is dedicated to editorial content (as opposed to ad content)? What is the editorial to ad content ratio of the magazine?

Answer Key

1. There are 95 advertisements in the magazine.
2. There are 76 full-page ads, 2 1/2-page ads, 10 1/3-page ads, 1 2/3-page ad, 0 1/4-page ads and 6 multi-page spreads (four 2-page, one 5-page and one 8-page).
3. Eighty (80) percent of the ads are full-page ads. [76 full-page ads / 95 ads total x 100 = 80%]
4. Two (2) percent of the ads are 1/2-page ads. [2 half-page ads / 95 ads total x 100 = 2.1 = 2%]
5. Twelve (12) percent of the ads are 1/3-page or 2/3-page ads. [10 (1/3-page ads) + 1 (2/3-page ad) = 11. 11 (1/3- and 2/3-page ads) / 95 ads total x 100 = 11.6 = 12%]
6. Zero (0) percent of the ads are 1/4-page ads. [0 / 95 x 100 = 0]
7. Six (6) percent of the ads are multi-page spreads. [6 multi-page spreads / 95 ads total x 100 = 6.3 = 6%.] Multi-page spreads account for 22 percent of the total number of ad pages. [8 pages (4 x 2 page) + 5 pages (1 x 5 pages) + 8 (1 x 8 pages) = 21 pages. 21 pages (multi) / 95 ads total x 100 = 22.1 = 22%]
8. The magazine is 206 pages in length (including front and back covers). Full-page ads account for 47 percent of the magazine's pages. [76 full-page ads + 21 pages (multi) = 97 pages. 97 full-page ads / 206 pages total x 100 = 47.1 = 47%]
9. Added together, the 1/2-page, 1/3-page, 2/3-page and 1/4-page ads represent 5 full pages. [2 x 1/2-page = 1 full page. (10 x 1/3) + (1 x 2/3) = 31/3 + 2/3 = 4 full pages. 1 + 4 = 5]
10. Ads account for 50 percent of the magazine's total pages. [97 ad pages + 5 ad pages = 102 ad pages. 102 ad pages / 206 total pages x 100 = 49.5 = 50%] Fifty (50) percent of the magazine is dedicated to editorial content. The editorial to ad content ratio of the magazine is 50:50.

Activity 46

Door Dividers

Count the number of doors in your home.

1. How many exterior doors are there in your home (front, back, garage, patio, etc.)?

2. How many interior doors are there in your home (bedroom, bathroom, closet, etc.)?

3. How many cabinet doors are there in your home (kitchen, bathroom, etc.)?

4. Which type of door is most numerous in your home? How many more doors of this type are there than of the other two types?

5. Which type of door is least numerous in your home? How many fewer doors of this type are there than of the other two types?

6. How many doors do you have in total in your home?

7. What percentage of the total number of doors do the exterior doors represent?

8. How many cupboard doors were in your kitchen? What percentage of your total number of cabinet doors does this represent?

9. If you had twice as many exterior doors, three times as many interior doors and four times as many cupboard doors, how many doors would you have in total in your home?

10. If there were 1/2 as many exterior doors, 1/3 as many interior or doors, and 1/4 as many cupboard doors in your home, how many doors would you have in total?

Answer Key

1. There are 16 exterior doors in my home.

2. There are 15 interior doors in my home.

3. There are 71 cabinet doors in my home.

4. In my home, the cabinet doors are most numerous. [71>15; 71>16] There are 55 more cabinet doors than exterior doors. [71 - 16 = 55] There are 56 more cabinet doors than interior doors. [71 - 15 = 56]

5. In my home, interior doors are the least numerous. [15<16; 15<71.] There are 56 fewer interior doors than cabinet doors. [71 - 15 = 56] There is one less interior door than exterior door. [16 - 15 = 1]

6. In total, there are 102 doors in my home. (16 + 15 + 71 = 102]

7. The exterior doors represent 15% of the total number of doors in my home. [16 (number of exterior doors) / 102 (total number of doors) = 0.157. 0.157 x 100 =16 (rounded up from 15.7)]

8. There are 33 cupboard doors in my kitchen. This represents 47% of the total number of cabinet doors in my home. [33 (number of kitchen cabinet doors) / 71 (total number of cupboard doors) = 0.4647. 0.4647 x 100 = 47 (rounded up from 46.47)]

9. If I had twice as many exterior doors, three times as many interior doors and four times as many cupboard doors, there would be 361 doors in my home in total. [(2 x 16 exterior doors) + (3 x 15 interior doors) + (4 x 71 cupboard doors) = 32 + 45 + 284 = 361]

10. If there were 1/2 as many exterior doors, 1/3 as many interior doors, and 1/4 as many cupboard doors in my home, there would be 31 doors in total. [(1/2 x 16/1 exterior doors) + (1/3 x 15/1 interior doors) + (1/4 x 71/1 cupboard doors) = 8 + 5 + 18 (rounded up from 17.75) = 31]

Newspaper Numbers

Pick up a copy of a newspaper.

1. How many sections are in the newspaper? What are they?
2. How many pages are in each section?
3. Arrange the sections according to page number in ascending order.
4. How many pages are in the entire newspaper?
5. What is the largest section? What is the smallest section? What is the difference between the largest and the smallest sections?
6. For what percentage of the newspaper does the largest section account?
7. For what percentage of the newspaper does the smallest section account?
8. What is the mean number of pages per section?
9. What is the median number of pages per section?
10. If you eliminate the largest section and the smallest section, what happens to the average number of pages per section?

Answer Key

1. There are 14 sections in the newspaper, The Saturday Star, Ontario Edition. The sections in the newspaper are: A: News; B: Sports; C: Classified; D: Business; F: Wheels; G: Greater Toronto; H: Careers; J: Life; K: National Report; L: Travel; M: Word on the Street/Arts; N: New in Homes; P: Condo Living; R: Color Comics.

2. A = 32 pages; B = 20 pages; C = 32 pages; D = 8 pages; F = 38 pages; G = 8 pages; H = 12 pages; J = 24 pages; K = 8 pages; L = 28 pages; M = 20 pages; N = 26 pages; P = 20 pages; R = 6.

3. Wheels, 38; News, 32; Classified, 32; Travel, 28; New in Homes, 26; Life, 24; Sports, 20; Word on the Street/Arts, 20; Condo Living, 20; Careers, 12; Business, 8; Greater Toronto, 8; National Report, 8; Color Comics, 6.

4. There are 282 pages in the entire newspaper. [32 + 20 + 32 + 8 + 38 + 8 + 12 + 24 + 8 + 28 + 20 + 26 + 20 + 6 = 282]

5. The largest section is F (Wheels) with 38 pages. The smallest section is R (Color Comics) with 6. The difference between the largest section and the smallest section is 32 pages. [38 (largest section) - 6 (smallest section) = 32]

6. The largest section accounts for 14 percent of the newspaper. [38 pages (largest section) / 282 pages (total) x 100 = 13.48 = 14%]

7. The smallest section accounts for two (2) percent of the newspaper. [6 pages (smallest section) / 282 pages (total) x 100 = 2.13 = 2%]

8. The mean number of pages per section is 20. [282 (number of pages) / 14 (number of sections) = 20.14 = 20]

9. The median number of pages is 20. [38, 32, 32, 28, 26, 24, 20, 20, 20, 12, 8, 8, 6. 20 (one middle) + 20 (one middle) = 40 / 2 = 20]

10. If I eliminate the largest section and the smallest section, the average (mean) number of pages per section remains the same, at 20. [282 pages (total) - 38 pages (largest section) - 6 pages (smallest section) = 238 pages. 238 (adjusted pages) / 12 (sections remaining) = 19.8 = 20]

Activity 48

Cookie Counters

Look inside an already-opened bag of cookies.
(You are going to have to do some estimating in this activity.)

1. How many cookies are left in the bag?

2. How many rows of cookies does the bag hold? How many cookies are in a full row? How many cookies would a full bag contain?

3. How many cookies have already been eaten?

4. How many grams of cookies are in a full bag?

5. How many grams would each cookie weigh?

6. If you ate the remaining cookies, how many grams of cookie would you consume?

7. If you divided a full bag of cookies equally among your family members, how many whole cookies would each person get? How many whole cookies would the remainder be?

8. If you divided the remaining cookies equally among your family members, how many whole cookies would each person get? How many whole cookies would the remainder be?

9. If the youngest person in your family received one cookie after dinner each night, the next oldest person received two, the next oldest person received three, and so on, how many cookies would your family eat in a week? How many bags of cookies would you need to buy each week? (How many grams of cookie would you eat in a year?)

10. If each person in your family were allowed to eat his or her age in cookies each week, how many cookies would you need to supply your family this year? How many bags of cookies would you have to buy? (How many grams of cookie would you eat each month?)

Answer Key

1. There are 19 cookies left in the bag.

2. A bag of cookies holds three rows. There are 12 cookies in a full row. Therefore, a full bag would contain 36 cookies. [3 (rows of cookies) × 12 (cookies/row) = 36 (cookies/bag)]

3. Seventeen (17) cookies have already been eaten. [36 (cookies/bag) − 19 (cookies remaining) = 17 (cookies eaten)]

4. A full bag of cookies contains 350 grams.

5. Each cookie weighs 9.7 grams. [350 (grams/bag) / 36 (cookies/bag) = 9.7 (grams/cookie)]

6. If I ate the remaining cookies, I would consume 184.3 grams of cookie. [19 (cookies remaining) × 9.7 (grams/cookie) = 184.3 (grams)]

7. If I divided a full bag of cookies equally among my family members, each person would get seven (7) whole cookies. The remainder would be one (1) whole cookie. [36 (cookies/bag) / 5 (family members) = 7.2 = 7 (whole cookies). 0.2 (remainder) × 5 (family members) = 1]

8. If I divided the remaining cookies equally among my family members, each person would get three (3) whole cookies. The remainder would yield four (4) whole cookies. [19 (cookies remaining) / 5 (family members) = 3.8 = 3 (whole cookies). 0.8 (remainder) × 5 (family members) = 4]

9. If the youngest person in my family received one cookie after dinner each night, the next oldest person received two, the next oldest person received three, and so on, my family would eat 105 cookies in a week. We would need to buy three bags of cookies each week. (I would eat 14,123 grams of cookie in a year.) [1 (Stephanie) + 2 (Patrick) + 3 (Matthew) + 4 (Tracey) + 5 (Jonathan) = 15 (cookies/night) × 7 (nights/week) = 105 cookies/week. 105 (cookies/week) / 36 (cookies/bag) = 2.91 = 3 (bags of cookies). 4 (cookies/night) × 9.7 (grams/cookie) × 7 (nights/week) × 52 (weeks/year) = 14,123.2 = 14,123 (grams/year).]

10. If each person in my family were allowed to eat his or her age in cookies each week, we would need 5616 cookies to supply us for one year. We would have to buy 156 bags of cookies each year. (I would eat 1436 grams of cookie each month.) [9 (Stephanie) + 10 (Patrick) + 13 (Matthew) + 37 (Me) + 39 (Jonathan) = 108 (cookies/week). 108 (cookies/week) × 52 (weeks/year) = 5616 (cookies/year). 5616 (cookies/year) / 36 (cookies/bag) = 156 (bags/year). 37 (cookies/week) × 4 (weeks/month) × 9.7 (grams/cookie) = 1435.6 = 1436 (grams).]

TV Guiders

Look in the television guide. (To come up with exact figures in this exercise, you might have to match call letters, such as TSN, with their corresponding station numbers.)

1. How many different stations are broadcasting?

2. (a) Choose an early morning (a.m.) timeslot on Monday. How many stations are broadcasting? (b) Choose a late-night (p.m.) timeslot on Tuesday. How many stations are broadcasting? (c) How many stations are broadcasting in a popular afternoon time slot on Wednesday?

3. Subtract your answer in question 2(a) from your answer in question 2(c). What is the difference?

4. Assuming the same number of programs air every day during your time slot in question 2(c), how many shows will air at this time over the course of a week? A month? (Assume a month is four weeks.)

5. How many different stations do you watch regularly? How many stations do you watch occasionally? How many stations do you never watch?

6. What percentage of stations broadcasting do you watch regularly? What percentage of stations broadcasting do you watch occasionally? What percentage of stations broadcasting do you never watch?

7. Add together all the station numbers that are broadcasting in a popular evening timeslot today. What is the sum?

8. Divide your answer in question 7 by the number of stations that are broadcasting during the timeslot in question 7. What is the quotient?

9. Subtract the station number of the show you would most like to watch during the timeslot in question 7 from your answer in question 7. What is the difference?

10. Subtract all of the station numbers that are broadcasting in an early morning time slot tomorrow from your answer in question 7. What is the difference?

Answer Key

1. There are 74 "broadcast and cable channels" listed in my television guide.

2. (a) There are 12 stations broadcasting at 3:30 a.m. on Monday. (b) There are 34 stations broadcasting at 11:30 p.m. on Tuesday. (c) There are 63 stations broadcasting at 4:00 p.m. on Wednesday.

3. Subtracting my answer in question 2(a) from my answer in question 2(c) yields a difference of 51. [63 (question 2c) - 12 (question 2a) = 51.]

4. Assuming the same number of programs airs each day at 4:00 p.m., 441 shows will air during this time slot over the course of a week, and 1764 shows will air during this time slot over the course of a month. [63 programs/day x 7 days/week = 441. 441 programs/week x 4 weeks/month = 1,764.]

5. I watch 8 different stations regularly. I watch 15 stations occasionally. I never watch 51 stations. (74 - 8 - 15 = 51.)

6. I regularly watch 11 percent of stations broadcasting. [8 stations (regularly) / 74 stations (total) x 100 = 10.8 = 11%] I occasionally watch 20 percent of stations broadcasting. [15 stations (occasionally) / 74 stations (total) x 100 = 20.3 = 20%] I never watch 69 percent of stations broadcasting. [51 stations (never) / 74 stations (total) x 100 = 68.9 = 69%.]

7. Adding together all the station numbers that are broadcasting at 6:00 p.m. today yields a sum of 412. [2 + 11 + 12 + 3 + 4 + 7 + 9 + 10 + 11 + 13 + 6 + 41 + 17 + 23 + 25 + 29 + 36 + 47 + 49 + 57 = 412.]

8. Dividing my answer in question 7 by the number of stations that are broadcasting at 6:00 p.m. today yields a quotient of 20.6. [412 / 20 = 20.6]

9. Subtracting the station number of the show I would most like to watch at 6:00 p.m. today from my answer in question 7 yields a difference of 365. [412 - 47 = 365]

10. Subtracting all of the station numbers that are broadcasting at 4:00 a.m. tomorrow from my answer in question 7 yields a difference of 383. [412 - 29 = 383]

Activity 50

Timely Tabulations

Look at a watch or clock.

1. What time is it?
2. Express the time in three alternate ways.
3. How long have you been up?
4. How long is it until your bedtime?
5. What time was it one-half hour ago?
6. What time will it be one-half hour from now?
7. If you add 100 minutes to the time, what time would it be?
8. If you subtract 100 minutes from the time, what time would it be?
9. Think of a foreign country. What time is it in that country? (You might need to consult an atlas or a telephone directory to complete this question.)
10. How long did it take you to do this activity?

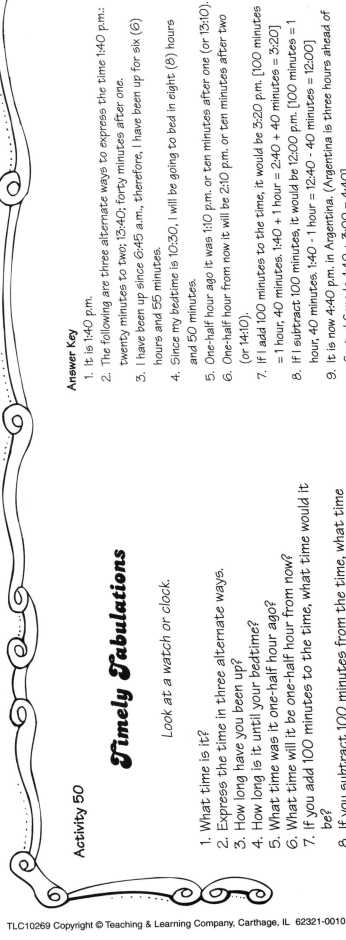

Answer Key

1. It is 1:40 p.m.
2. The following are three alternate ways to express the time 1:40 p.m.: twenty minutes to two; 13:40; forty minutes after one.
3. I have been up since 6:45 a.m., therefore, I have been up for six (6) hours and 55 minutes.
4. Since my bedtime is 10:30, I will be going to bed in eight (8) hours and 50 minutes.
5. One-half hour ago it was 1:10 p.m. or ten minutes after one (or 13:10).
6. One-half hour from now it will be 2:10 p.m. or ten minutes after two (or 14:10).
7. If I add 100 minutes to the time, it would be 3:20 p.m. [100 minutes = 1 hour, 40 minutes. 1:40 + 1 hour = 2:40 + 40 minutes = 3:20]
8. If I subtract 100 minutes, it would be 12:00 p.m. [100 minutes = 1 hour, 40 minutes. 1:40 - 1 hour = 12:40 - 40 minutes = 12:00]
9. It is now 4:40 p.m. in Argentina. (Argentina is three hours ahead of Central Canada. 1:40 + 3:00 = 4:40)
10. It is now 1:58 p.m. It took me 18 minutes to complete this activity. [1:58 - 1:40 = 18 minutes]

Serial Cereal

Take a box of cereal out of your kitchen cupboard.

1. Look on the front of the box. How many grams of cereal does the box contain?

2. Look on the information panel on the side of the cereal box. How many grams are in a single suggested serving (bowl)?

3. If you weren't feeling very hungry and ate only a half-serving, how many grams of cereal would you consume?

4. How much fat is in a single serving? If you had one-and-one-half bowls of cereal, how many grams of fat would you consume?

5. How many calories are in a serving? If you had two bowls of cereal, how many calories would you consume?

6. If you eat one bowl of cereal every day, how many grams of cereal will you eat in one week?

7. If you eat two bowls of cereal each day, how much cereal will you eat in a year?

8. Based on the suggested serving size, how many servings of cereal are in each box? (Round your answer to the nearest full serving.)

9. If each person in your family eats one bowl of cereal for breakfast, how many days will one box last?

10. Based on the one-bowl-a-day/person calculation in question 9, how many boxes of cereal will your family buy each year?

Answer Key

1. There are 775 grams of cereal in the box of cereal.

2. A single serving of cereal is 40 grams.

3. A half-serving of cereal is 20 grams. [40 (grams/serving) / 2 (or 40/1 × ½) = 20 grams]

4. There are 0.7 grams of fat per serving. I would consume 1.05 grams of fat in 1½ servings of cereal. [0.7 (grams of fat/serving) × 1.5 (servings) = 1.05 (or: 0.7+0.35=1.05)]

5. There are 390 calories in two servings of cereal. [195 calories per serving. 195 (calories/serving × 2 (servings) = 390 calories.]

6. I would eat 280 grams of cereal each week. [40 (grams/serving) × 7 (days/week) = 280 grams]

7. I would eat 4160 grams of cereal each year. [40 (grams/serving) × 2 (servings/day) × 7 days/week × 52 (weeks/year) = 29,120 grams (or 29.12 kilograms]

8. There are approximately 19 servings in each box of cereal. [775 (grams in box) / 40 (grams/serving) = 19.375 = 19]

9. A box of cereal would last my family four (4) days. [5 (people in family) × 40 (grams/serving) = 200 (grams/day). 775 (grams in box) / 200 (grams/day) = 4 days (rounded up from 3.875) Or: 19 (servings/box) / 5 (servings/family/day) = 4 days (rounded up from 3.8)]

10. My family would have to buy 91 boxes of cereal per year. [365 (days/year) / 4 (days/box) = 91 boxes (rounded up from 91.25)]

Activity 52

Telephone Times

Write down your telephone number (including area code).

1. Express this number in numerical form.
2. Write out this number in words.
3. Assign a place value to each digit in this number.
4. If you add the digits in your telephone number together, what is your addition telephone total?
5. Subtract the area code from your addition telephone total. What is your new addition telephone total?
6. Multiply the digits in your telephone number together. (Substitute the number one for any zeros.) What is your multiplication telephone total?
7. Divide your multiplication telephone total by the number of digits in your telephone number. What is the quotient?
8. Divide your multiplication telephone total by your addition telephone total in question 4. What is the quotient?
9. Multiply your area code by your answer in question 5. (Substitute the number one for any zeros.) What is your new multiplication telephone total?
10. Compare your telephone totals as a class. Which students have the highest addition and multiplication telephone totals in your class? Which students have the lowest?

Answer Key

(800) 555-1234

1. 8,005,551,234
2. Eight billion, five million, five hundred fifty-one thousand, two hundred thirty four.
3. Eight billions; zero one hundred millions; zero ten millions; five millions; five one hundred thousands; five ten thousands; one thousand; two hundreds; three tens; four ones.
4. My addition telephone total is 33. [8 + 0 + 0 + 5 + 5 + 5 + 1 + 2 + 3 + 4 = 33]
5. My addition telephone total, minus the area code, is 25. [33 - 8 - 0 - 0 = 25]
6. My multiplication telephone total is 24,000. [8 × 1 × 1 × 5 × 5 × 5 × 1 × 2 × 3 × 4 = 24,000]
7. When divided by the number of digits in my telephone number; my multiplication telephone total is 2400. [24,000 / 10 (no. of digits) = 2400]
8. When I divide my multiplication telephone total by my addition telephone total in Question #4, I get a quotient of 727. [24,000 / 33 = 727 (rounded down from 727.3]
9. By multiplying my area code by my answer in question 5, I get a new multiplication telephone total of 20,000. [800 (area code) x 25 (answer from 5) = 20,000]

Toilet Turbulence

1. On average, how many times do you flush a toilet each day?

2. If each flush requires five (5) gallons of water, how much water do you use each day?

3. How much water do you flush down the toilet each week? Each month?

4. How much water do you flush down the toilet each year?

5. If each person in your family flushes the toilet as frequently as you do, how much water does your family use each day?

6. How much water does your family flush down the toilet each week? Each month?

7. How much water does your family flush down the toilet each year?

8. If the kids in your family flush the toilet twice as much as you did in question 2, and the adults in your family flush the toilet three times as much as you did in question 2, how much water does your family use each day?

9. If the kids in your family flush the toilet ½ as many times as you did in question 2, and the adults in your family flush the toilet ⅓ as many times as you did in question 2, how much water does your family flush down the toilet every day?

10. If each person on your street or block flushes the toilet as often as you did in question 2, how much water do the people on your street or block flush down the toilet each day? (Estimate the number of people living on your street or block.)

Answer Key

1. On average, I flush the toilet six (6) times each day.

2. If each flush uses five (5) gallons of water, I use 30 gallons of water each day. [6 flushes/day x 5 gallons/flush = 30 gallons]

3. I flush 210 gallons of water down the toilet each week. [30 gallons/day x 7 days/week = 210 gallons/week] I flush 840 gallons of water down the toilet each month. [210 gallons/week x 4 weeks/month = 840 gallons/month]

4. I flush 10,950 gallons of water down the toilet each year. [30 gallons/day x 365 days/year = 10,950 gallons/year]

5. If each person in my family flushes the toilet as frequently as I do, my family uses 150 gallons of water each day. [30 gallons/day x 5 family members = 150 gallons/day]

6. Each week, my family flushes 1050 gallons of water down the toilet. [150 gallons/day x 7 days/week = 1050] Each month, my family flushes 4200 gallons of water down the toilet. [1050 gallons/week x 4 weeks/month = 4200 gallons/month]

7. Each year, my family flushes 54,750 gallons of water down the toilet. [150 gallons/day x 365 days/year = 54,750 gallons/year]

8. If the kids in my family flush the toilet twice as much as I did in question 2, and the adults in my family flush the toilet three times as much as I did in question 2, my family uses 360 gallons of water each day. [30 gallons/day x 2 x 3 kids = 180 gallons/day. 30 gallons/day x 3 x 2 adults = 180 gallons/day. 180 gallons + 180 gallons = 360 gallons/day]

9. If the kids in my family flush the toilet ½ as many times as I did in question 2, and the adults in my family flush the toilet ⅓ as many times as I did in question 2, my family flushes 65 gallons of water down the toilet every day. [30 gallons/day x ½ x 3 kids = 45 gallons/day. 30 gallons/day x ⅓ x 2 adults = 20 gallons/day. 45 gallons/day (kids) + 20 gallons/day (adults) = 65 gallons/day]

10. If each person on my block flushes the toilet as often as I did in question 2, the people on my block flush 1800 gallons of water down the toilet each day. [30 gallons/day x 15 houses x 4 occupants/house = 1800 gallons/day]

Activity 54

Menu Math

Make up a menu. Include three different appetizers (starters), three different entrées (main courses), three different side dishes, three different desserts and three different drinks. Put a price beside each menu item. (Do not duplicate prices in a single category.)

1. Choose your favorite meal from your menu. Include one item from each menu category. What is the price of your meal?

2. Ask a member of your family to choose his or her favorite meal from your menu. Include one item from each menu category. What is the price of his or her meal?

3. In questions 1 and 2, whose meal was more expensive? How much more expensive?

4. What is the most expensive meal combination on your menu? What is the price of this meal combination?

5. What is the least expensive meal combination on your menu? What is the price of this meal combination?

6. How much more expensive than your meal was the most expensive meal? How much less expensive than your meal was the least expensive meal?

7. Add another side dish to the meal in question 4. What is the new price of the meal?

8. Take the appetizer away from the meal in question 5. What is the new price of the meal?

9. If someone ordered all of the side dishes, the least expensive entrée and the most expensive drink, how much would he or she have to pay?

10. If two people wanted to split the cost of the most expensive appetizer and the most expensive dessert on this menu, how much would each person have to pay?

Answer Key

1. My favorite meal on this menu is potato skins, baked chicken, French fries, apple pie and cola. The price of my favorite meal is $20.50.
[$4.50 + $9.00 + $2.00 + $3.50 + $1.50 = $20.50.]

2. My son's favorite meal on this menu is shrimp cocktail, roast beef, french fries, cheesecake and cola. The price of his favorite meal is $23.00. [$5.50 + $10.00 + $2.00 + $4.00 + $1.50 = $23.00.]

3. In questions 1 and 2, my son's meal was $2.50 more expensive than mine. [$23.00 - $20.50 = $2.50.]

4. The most expensive meal combination on this menu is shrimp cocktail, roast beef, soup, cheesecake and cola. The price of this meal is $24.00. [$5.50 + $10.00 + $3.00 + $4.00 + $1.50 = $24.00.]

5. The least expensive meal combination on this menu is vegetable platter, broiled fish, French fries, ice cream and juice. The price of this meal is $18.00. [$4.00 + $8.00 + $2.00 + $3.00 + $1.00 = $18.00.]

6. The most expensive meal was $3.50 more than my meal. [$24.00 - $20.50 = $3.50.] The least expensive meal was $2.50 less expensive than my meal. [$20.50 - $18.00 = $2.50.]

7. If I add a salad to the meal in Question #4, the new price of the meal is $26.50. [$24.00 + $2.50 = $26.50.]

8. If I take the appetizer away from the meal in question #5, the new price of the meal is $14.00. [$18.00 - $4.00 = $14.00.]

9. If someone ordered all of the side dishes, the least expensive entrée and the most expensive drink, he or she would have to pay $17.00. [[(broiled fish) $8.00 + (French fries) $2.00 + (soup) $3.00 + (salad) $2.50 + (cola) $1.50 = $17.00.]

10. If two people wanted to split the cost of the most expensive appetizer and the most expensive dessert on this menu, each person would have to pay $4.75. [[(shrimp cocktail) $5.50 + (cheesecake) $4.00 = $9.50. $9.50 / 2 = $4.75.]

Appetizers	
Potato skins	$4.50
Shrimp cocktail	$5.50
Vegetable platter	$4.00

Entrées	
Broiled fish	$8.00
Baked chicken	$9.00
Roast beef	$10.00

Side Dishes	
French fries	$2.00
Soup	$3.00
Salad	$2.50

Desserts	
Apple pie	$3.50
Cheesecake	$4.00
Ice cream	$3.00

Drinks	
Milk	$1.25
Juice	$1.00
Cola	$1.50

Pizza Percentages

Yea! Your family is going to have pizza for dinner.

1. How many pieces of pizza does each person in your family normally eat in one meal? How many pieces of pizza does your family eat in total in one meal?

2. If a small pizza has six (6) pieces, a medium has eight (8) pieces, and a large has 12 pieces, what is the minimum number of pizzas you will need to feed your family (with as few leftover pieces as possible)?

3. How many pizzas will you need to buy if you want enough pizza left over to feed your family dinner tomorrow? (Again, find the combination that requires the fewest number of pizzas with the least number of slices left over.)

4. If a small costs $9, a medium costs $12 and a large costs $15, how much will it cost to buy the pizzas in question 2?

5. Is there a better deal? In other words can you get more pizza for the same or less money with a different combination than the one in Question #4?

6. If you could buy one pizza and get a second pizza of the same size for free, how much will it cost to buy enough pizza to feed your family for one meal?

7. How many toppings do you want on each of your pizzas? If each pizza comes "standard" with three toppings and each additional topping costs $.50, how much extra will appear on your pizza bill? What is the new total of your pizza bill?

8. If everyone in your family wants a pop with their pizza and each pop costs $1.25, how much extra will your beverages add to your pizza bill? What is your total pizza bill?

9. If you need to have the pizza delivered and it costs

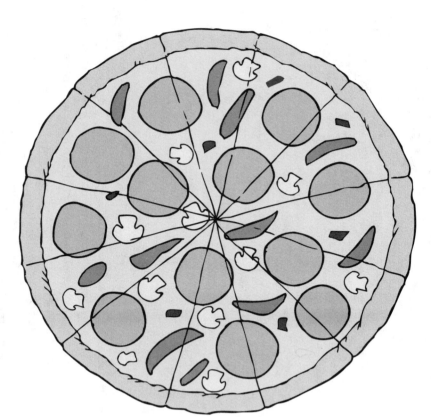

$.50/mile for delivery, how much extra will you have to pay the pizza delivery person when he or she arrives at your door? How will this affect the price of your pizza? (Estimate how many miles you are from the closest—or your favorite—pizza parlor.)

10. If you have to tip the delivery person 10% of your total pizza order, how much will the tip be? What is the total cost of your pizza night?

Answer Key

1. In my family, Jonathan and I eat four (4) pieces of pizza each, Matthew and Patrick eat three (3) pieces of pizza each and Stephanie eats two (2) pieces of pizza. In total, our family eats 16 pieces of pizza in one meal. [4 × 2 = 8. 3 × 2 = 6. 1 × 2 = 2. 8 + 6 + 2 = 16]

2. If a small has six (6) pieces, a medium has eight (8) pieces, and a large has 12 pieces, the minimum number of pizzas we will need to feed our family (with as few leftover pieces as possible) is 2: two mediums. [1 medium (8 slices) + 1 medium (8 slices) = 16 slices]

3. We will need to buy 3 pizzas (two larges and one medium) if we want enough pizza left over to feed our family dinner tomorrow. [16 pieces × 2 nights = 32 pieces. 1 large (12 slices) + 1 large (12 slices) + 1 medium (8 slices) = 32 pieces]

4. If a small costs $9, a medium costs $12 and a large costs $15, it will cost $24 to buy enough pizza to feed our family for one night. [2 (medium pizza) × $12 = $24]

5. There is a better deal. We could get one large pizza and one small pizza for the same price - $24 - and have two slices left over. [$15 (1 large) + $9 (1 small) = $24. 12 slices (large) + 6 slices (small) = 18 slices. 18 slices (new combo) - 16 slices (old combo) = 2 slices]

6. If we could buy one pizza and get the second pizza of the same size for free, it will cost $12 to buy enough pizza to feed our family for one meal. [$12 (medium) + $0 (medium) = $12]

7. We want extra cheese and pepperoni on our first pizza, and onions, green olives, hot peppers, bacon and mushrooms on our second pizza. If each pizza comes "standard" with three toppings, we will need to buy two extra toppings for our second pizza. $1.00 extra will appear on our pizza bill for these two toppings. [$.50 + $.50 = $1.] The new total of our pizza bill is $25. [$24 + $1 = $25]

8. If everyone in our family wants a pop with their pizza and each pop costs $1.25, our beverages will add an extra $6.25 to our pizza bill. [$1.25 per beverage × 5 family members = $6.25] Our total pizza bill is now $31.25. [$24 (2 mediums) + $1 (extra toppings) + $6.25 (5 beverages) = $31.25]

9. If we need to have the pizza delivered and it costs $.50/mile for delivery, we will have to pay an extra $3 for delivery. [$.50 per mile × 6 miles = $3] This will increase our total pizza bill to $34.25. [$24 (2 mediums) + $1 (extra toppings) + $6.25 (beverages) + $3.00 (delivery) = $34.25]

10. If we have to tip the delivery person 15% of our total pizza order, the tip will be $5. [$34.25 × .15 = 5.1 = $5] This will bring the total of our pizza night bill to $39.25. [$34.25 (2 medium pizzas with two extra toppings, five beverages, delivery) + $5 (delivery person's tip) = $39.25]

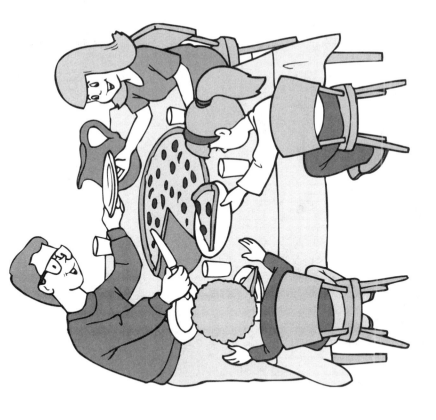

Utilitarianism

Ask a parent if you can look at one of your monthly electric bills. (If you do not receive a monthly utility bill, ask a friend or relative to relate the information printed on his or her bill.)

1. What was the amount of the bill?
2. How much electricity did your family use in one month?
3. If you cut your consumption by one third, how much money would you save each month? (Look at your bill to determine the price of a kilowatt of power.)
4. How many kilowatts of power do you use over the course of a year? How expensive is your annual electric bill?
5. If your fridge uses 3.3 kilowatts of power each day, how much does it cost each month to keep your food cold? How much does it cost to run your fridge for a year?
6. If it costs $.02 to run your TV for an hour, how much power does your TV use?
7. How many hours of TV do you watch each day? How much does it cost to run your TV each month?
8. If you watched 1/2 hour less of TV each day, what would the TV portion of your monthly electric bill cost? How much would you save over the course of a year?
9. If it takes 1.5 kilowatts of power to run your dishwasher for an hour, and each dishwashing cycle takes 1 1/2 hours, how much does it cost to run your dishwasher for a week? How much power does it take to run your dishwasher each year?
10. How much money could you save each year on your electric bill if you did the dishes by hand?

Answer Key

1. The amount of our last electric bill was $117.60.
2. My family used 1470 kilowatts of power last month.
3. If we cut our consumption by one third, we would save $39.20 each month. [1470 kilowatt hours/month x 1/3 x $.08/kilowatt hour = $39.20 or $117.60 x 1/3 = $39.20]
4. We use 17,640 kilowatt hours of power each year. [1470 kilowatt hours/month x 12 months = 17,640] Our annual electric bill amounts to $1411.20. [17,640 kilowatt hours/year x $.08/kilowatt hours = $1411.20 or $117.60/month x 12 months = $1411.20]
5. If our fridge uses 3.3 kilowatt hours of power each day, it costs us $7.92 each month to keep our food cold. [3.3 kilowatt hours/day x 30 days/month = 99 kilowatt hours/month. 99 kilowatt hours/month x $.08/kilowatt hour = $7.92] It costs us $95.04 to run our fridge for a year. [$7.92/month x 12 = $95.04]
6. If it costs $.02 to run our TV for an hour, our TV uses 0.25 kilowatts per hour. [$.02 / $.08 = 0.25 kilowatt/hour]
7. My family watches two (2) hours of TV each day. It costs $1.20 to run our TV each month. [2 hours TV/day x 30 days/month = 60 hours TV/month. 60 hours TV/month x $.02/hour = $1.20/month.]
8. If we watched 1/2 hour less TV each day, the TV portion of our monthly electric bill would cost $.90. [2 hours - .5 hour = 1.5 hours. 1.5 hours TV/day x 30 x $.02 = $.90] We would save $3.60 over the course of a year. [$.90/month x 12 = $10.80. $1.20 x 12 = $14.40. $14.40 - $10.80 = $3.60]
9. If it takes 1.5 kilowatt hours of power to run our dishwasher for an hour, and each dishwashing cycle takes 1 1/2 hours, it costs $1.26 to run our dishwasher for a week. [1.5 kilowatts/hour x 1.5 hours/cycle x 7 days/week x $.08/kilowatt hour = $1.26/week] Our dishwasher uses 821.25 kilowatt hours of power per year. [1.5 kilowatt/hour x 1.5 hours/cycle x 365 cycles/year = 821.25 kilowatt hours/year]
10. If we washed the dishes by hand, we could save $65.52 each year on the electric bill. [$1.26/week x 52 weeks/year = $65.52/year]

Activity 57

Wordly Wise

Choose a chapter book.

1. Pick a page somewhere near the middle of the book. How many words does the first line of that page contain?

2. How many words does a line near the middle of the page contain? How many words does the last line of the page contain?

3. What is the average number of words per line based on your word counts in questions 1 and 2?

4. Complete word counts for three more lines on the page. What is the average of the six lines? How does this average compare to your answer in question 3?

5. How many lines are on the page?

6. Based on your answer to question 4, estimate how many words will appear on the page.

7. Count the number of words on the page. How many words are on the page?

8. How does your answer in question 7 compare to your estimate in question 6?

9. How many pages of text are in the book?

10. Based on your estimate in question 6, approximately how many words are there in the book? Based on your actual count in question 7, approximately how many words are there in the book? What is the difference between the two estimates? How many pages does this represent using the two words/page estimates?

Answer Key

1. The first line on the page contains 9 words.

2. There are 11 words on a line near the middle of the page. The last line on the page contains 10 words.

3. The average number of words per line, based on my word counts in questions 1 and 2, is 10. [9 + 11 + 10 = 30 words. 30 words / 3 lines = 10 words/line]

4. A second survey of three lines yielded the same number of words per line as the first survey: 9, 11 and 10. The average of the six lines is 10 words. This is the same as my answer in question 3. [9 + 11 + 10 + 30 = 60 words. 60 words / 6 lines = 10 words/line]

5. There are 26 lines on the page.

6. Based on my answer to question 4, there will be an estimated 260 words on the page. [10 words/line × 26 lines/page = 260 words/page]

7. There are, in fact, 238 words on the page.

8. My answer in question 7 is less than my estimate in question 6. There are 22 fewer words per page than I had estimated based on my words/line trials. [260 words/page (estimate) - 238 words/page (actual) = 22 words]

9. There are 294 pages of text in the book.

10. Based on the estimate in question 6, there are approximately 76,440 words in the book. [260 words/page × 294 pages = 76,440 words] Based on the actual count in question 7, there are approximately 69,972 words in the book. [238 words/page × 294 pages = 69,972 words] The difference between the two estimates is [76,440 (estimate in question 6) - 69,972 words (estimate in question 7) = 6,468 words] This represents 25 extra pages using the estimate in question 6 [6468 words / 260 words/page = 24.88 = 25 pages] and 27 pages extra using the estimate in question 7. [6468 words / 238 words/page = 27.18 = 27 pages]

Zip Code Code

1. What is your zip code?*
2. Express your zip code as a number.
3. What is your zip code number in words?
4. Assign a place value to each of the digits in your zip code number.
5. Arrange the digits of your zip code in ascending order.
6. Arrange the digits of your zip code in descending order.
7. Add the digits of your zip code together. What is the sum?
8. Multiply the digits of your zip code together. (Substitute your age for any zeros.) What is the product?
9. Divide the product in question 8 by the number of digits in your zip code. What is the quotient?
10. Subtract the quotient in question 9 from the product in question 8. What is the difference?

*If your zip or postal code has letters as well as or in place of numbers, substitute numbers for letters according to the following alphanumeric code: A=1, B=2, C=3 . . . Z=26.

Answer Key

1. My postal code is LOC 1GO, or in alphanumeric code: 12 O 3 17 O.
2. As a number, my postal code is 1,203,170.
3. In words, my postal code is one million, two hundred three thousand, one hundred seventy.
4. The place value of each of the digits in my postal code is: 1 million, 2 hundred thousands, O ten thousands, 3 thousands, 1 one hundred, 7 tens, O ones.
5. In ascending order, the digits in my postal code read: O O 1 3 7 12.
6. In descending order, the digits in my postal code read: 12 7 3 1 O O.
7. Adding the digits of my postal code together yields a sum of 23. [12 + O + 3 + 1 + 7 + O = 23]
8. Multiplying the digits of my postal code together (substituting my age for any zeros) yields a product of 344,988. [12 × 37 × 3 × 1 × 7 × 37 = 344,988]
9. Dividing the product in question 8 by the number of digits in my postal code yields a quotient of 57,498. [344,988 / 6 = 57,498]
10. Subtracting the quotient in question 9 from the product in question 8 yields a difference of 287,499. [344,988 - 57,489 = 287,499]

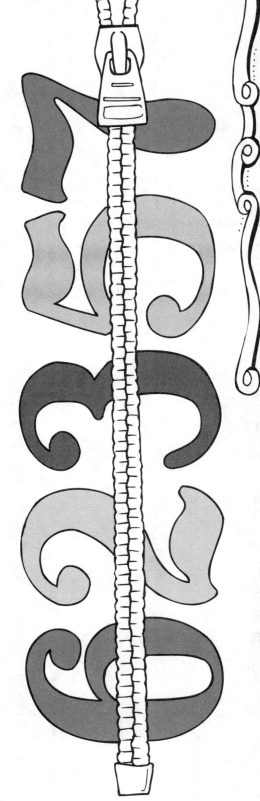

Activity 59

Laundry Loads

Empty your laundry hamper.

1. How many articles of clothing were in the hamper?

2. Sort the dirty laundry. How many white articles were in the hamper? How many dark articles? How many colored articles?

3. How many shirts were in the hamper? How many pairs of pants/shorts? How many socks were in the hamper? How many pairs of underwear?

4. What type of laundry article is most numerous? What is the least numerous? What is the ratio of most to least numerous articles of laundry?

5. For what percentage of your dirty laundry do your socks account?

6. If you took away all the socks and underwear, how many articles of clothing would be left?

7. Multiply the number of articles in your laundry hamper by the number of people in your household. What is the product?

8. If each person in your household soils twice as much laundry as the product in question 7 in a week, how many articles of clothing will your family soil in a month?

9. If the pile of clothing in my hamper represents three days worth of laundry, how many articles of clothing do you soil per day?

10. If this pile of clothing represents four days worth of laundry, how many articles of clothing will you soil in a week?

Answer Key

1. There were 65 articles of clothing in my laundry hamper.

2. There were 31 white articles, 16 dark articles and 18 colored articles in the hamper.

3. There were 12 shirts, 5 pairs of pants/shorts, 16 pairs of underwear and 32 socks in the hamper.

4. In my laundry hamper, socks are the most numerous and pants/shorts are the least numerous. Socks outnumber pants/shorts 32:5.

5. Socks account for 49 percent of my dirty laundry. [32 (socks) / 65 (total clothing articles) x 100 = 49.23 = 49%.]

6. If I took away all the socks and underwear, there would be 17 articles of clothing left in my laundry hamper. [32 (socks) + 16 (underwear) = 48. 65 - 48 = 17.]

7. Multiplying the number of articles in my laundry hamper by the number of people in my household yields a product of 325. [65 (number of articles in hamper) x 5 (number of people in household) = 325.]

8. If each person in my household soils twice as much laundry as the product in question 7 in a week, my family will soil 2600 articles of clothing in a month. [325 (articles of laundry) x 2 x 4 (weeks/month) = 2600.]

9. If the pile of clothing in my hamper represents three days worth of laundry, I soil 22 articles of clothing each day. [65 (articles of clothing) / 3 (days) = 21.6 = 22.]

10. If this pile of clothing represents four days worth of laundry, I will soil 112 articles of clothing in a week. [65 (articles of clothing) / 4 (days) = 16.25 = 16 (articles of clothing per day). 16 (articles of clothing/day) x 7 (days/week) = 112 (articles of clothing/week).]

The Re-Cycle

Look in your recycling bin. (If you don't have a recycling bin, ask a friend or a relative to supply you with the data for this activity. If all else fails, substitute fantasy for fact!)

1. How many paper items are in your recycling bin? (If there are hundreds of papers in your bin, you can guesstimate!)
2. How many plastic items are in your recycling bin?
3. How many metal items are in your recycling bin?
4. How many glass items are in your recycling bin?
5. How many recyclable items are in your recycling bin?
6. Which item is most numerous in your bin? Which item is least numerous in your bin? How many more of the most numerous item are there than of the least numerous item? What is the ratio of most numerous to least numerous items in your bin?
7. Express the number of paper items in your bin as a percentage of the whole. What is the ratio of paper to plastic items in your bin?
8. Express the number of plastic items in your bin as a percentage of the whole. What is the ratio of plastic to metal items in your bin?
9. Express the number of metal items in your bin as a percentage of the whole. What is the ratio of metal to glass items in your bin?
10. Express the number of glass items in your bin as a percentage of the whole. What is the ratio of glass to paper items in your bin?

To check the accuracy of your percentage calculations, add the first answers to questions 7, 8, 9 and 10 together. If the sum of these numbers is 100 percent, then your calculations are probably accurate.

Answer Key

1. There are approximately 300 paper items in my recycling bin.
2. There are 5 plastic items in my recycling bin.
3. There are 11 metal items in my recycling bin.
4. There are 2 glass items in my recycling bin.
5. There are 318 recyclable items in my bin altogether. [300 + 5 + 11 + 2 = 318.]
6. The most numerous recycling item in my bin is paper. The least numerous recycling item in my bin is glass. There are 298 more paper items in my bin than plastic items. [300 paper (most numerous) - 2 glass (least numerous) = 298.] The ratio of most numerous to least numerous items in my bin is 150:1. [300/2. 300/2 = 150. 2/2 = 1. 150:1.]
7. Ninety-four percent of the items in my recycling bin are paper. [300 paper items / 318 total items x 100 = 94.3= 94%.] The ratio of paper to plastic items in my bin is 60:1. [300:5. 300/5 = 60. 5/5 = 1. 60:1.]
8. Two percent of the items in my recycling bin are plastic. [5 plastic items / 318 total items x 100 = 1.6 = 2%.] The ratio of plastic to metal items in my bin is 5:11.
9. Three percent of the items in my recycling bin are metal. [11 metal items / 318 total items x 100 = 3.5 = 3%.] The ratio of metal to glass items in my bin is 11:2.
10. One percent of the items in my recycling bin are glass. [2 glass items / 318 total items x 100 = 0.6 = 1%.] The ratio of glass to paper items in my bin is 1:150. [2:300. 2/2 = 1. 300/2 = 150. 1:150.]

Activity 61

Phonebook Fun

Open a telephone book to a page roughly in the middle.

1. Add the numbers at the top of each column on the left-hand page together. What is the sum?

2. Add the numbers at the top of each column on the right-hand page together. What is the sum?

3. Which page sum is greater? Subtract the greater sum from the lesser sum. What is the difference?

4. What is the average of the numbers across the top of the two pages? What number is closest to the average?

5. Add the numbers at the bottom of each column on the left-hand page together. What is the sum?

6. Add the numbers at the bottom of each column on the right-hand page together. What is the sum?

7. Which page sum is greater? Subtract the greater sum from the lesser sum. What is the difference?

8. What is the average of the numbers across the bottom of the two pages? What number is closest to the average?

9. How many listings are in the left-hand column?

10. Based on your answer to question 9, approximately how many listings are on the two-page spread?

Catalog Calculations

Look in a catalog.

1. Choose an expensive new outfit for school. Money is no object. Include shoes, a top and a bottom. What are the prices of the individual items? What is the total for the three items?

2. Assume you have a budget of $125.00. Choose an outfit to fit your budget. Include shoes, a top and a bottom. What are the prices of the individual items? What is the total? How much change would you have?

3. How much more expensive is your outfit in question 1 than your outfit in question 2?

4. If the shoes you chose in question 1 were on sale for 15% off, how much would you save? How much would they cost? What would be the new price of your complete outfit?

5. Choose a new coat and a pair of boots. What is the least expensive combination possible? What is the most expensive?

6. If you receive $5.00 a week for allowance, how long will it take you to save enough money to buy your favorite recreational equipment item advertised in the catalog?

7. Make a birthday wish list of 10 items from the catalog. How much money would you need to buy every item on the list? What is the average price of an item on your list?

8. If you received $23 from each of your relatives (parents, grandparents, brothers, sisters, aunts, uncles, cousins) for your birthday, how much money would you have in total? Would it be enough to purchase all of the items on your wish list in question 7?

9. Look through the catalog and choose a piece of jewellery for someone you love. If you were given $19 toward your purchase, how much more would you have to spend or how much change would you receive?

10. If you had $45 dollars to spend, what item would you buy for your best friend? How much change would you get after making your purchase?

Answer Key

1. When money was no object, the catalog items that I chose were: shoes: $99.99; top: $59.99; bottom: $34.99. The total for the three items is $194.97. [$99.99 + $59.99 + $34.99 = $194.97]

2. When I had a budget of $125, the catalog items that I chose were: shoes: $49.99; top: $19.99; bottom: $34.99. The total for the three items is $104.97. [$49.99 +$19.99 +$34.99 = $104.97] I will receive $20.03 in change. [$125.00 - $104.97 = $20.03]

3. My outfit in question 1 is $90 more than my outfit in question 2. [$194.97 - $104.97 = $90.00]

4. If the shoes I chose in question 1 were on sale for 15% off, they would cost $85. I would save $15. [$99.99 x .15 = 14.99. $99.99 - $14.99 = $85.] My complete outfit would cost $109.97. [$194.97 - $15 = $179.97]

5. The least expensive new coat and boots combination is $138.98. [$88.99 (coat) + $49.99 (boots) = $138.98.] The most expensive new coat and boots combination is $299.98. [$249.99 (coat) + $49.99 (boots) = $299.98]

6. If I receive $5.00 a week for allowance, it will take me 40 weeks to save enough money to buy my favorite recreational equipment item advertised in the catalog. [$199.99 (purchase price) / $5.00/week allowance = 39.99 = 40 weeks]

7. I would need $1639.90 to buy all 10 catalog items on my birthday wish list. [$199.99 + 109.99 + 179.99 + 549.99 + 79.99 + 79.99 + 79.99 + 79.99 + 99.99 + 179.99 = $1639.90.] The average price of an item on my list is $163.99. [$1639.90 / 10 items = $163.99]

8. If I received $23 from each of my relatives for my birthday, I would have $184 in total. [$23 (parents); $23 (parents-in-law); $23 (brother/family); $23 (sister-in-law/family); $23 (brother-in-law/family); $23 (aunt); $23 (aunt/family); $23 (aunt/family). $23 x 8 = $184] I would not have enough money to buy all of the items on my wish list in question 7. I would be $1455 short. [$1639 - $184 = $1455]

9. I would choose a necklace priced at $599.99. If I were given $19 toward my purchase, I would have to spend $580.99 more. [$599.99 - $19.00 = $580.99]

10. If I had $45 dollars to spend, I would buy a $39.99 item for my best friend. I would receive $5.01 change after making my purchase. [$45.00 - $39.99 = $5.01]

Activity 63

Bar Code Bonanza

Look at the bar codes on five products in your home. (The bar code is the small rectangular pattern of stripes found on the back or bottom of most products. There are generally two sets of five numbers under the bar. Ignore the smaller numbers that appear on either side of the bar.)

1. List the five 10-number bar codes from lowest to highest.

2. Subtract the lowest bar code number from the highest bar code number. What is the difference?

3. Subtract the second-highest bar code number from the highest bar code number. What is the difference? Express this number in standard form.

4. Add the two lowest bar code numbers together. What is the sum? Express this number in place values.

5. Subtract your answer in question 3 from your answer in question 2. What is the difference?

6. Using just the left-hand set of five numbers, add the bar codes together. What is the sum?

7. What is the average of the left-hand set of numbers? What number is closest to this number? What number is furthest from this number?

8. Using just the right-hand set of five numbers, add the bar codes together. What is the sum?

9. What is the average of the right-hand set of numbers? What number is closest to this number? What number is furthest from this number?

10. Subtract the higher bar code total from the lower bar code total. What is the difference?

Answer Key

1. 1,556,117,426; 6,038,365,844; 6,222,901,004; 6,520,377,683; 6,810,008,421

2. The difference between the highest bar code number and the lowest bar code number is 5,253,890,995. [6,810,008,421 - 1,556,117,426 = 5,253,890,995]

3. The difference between highest bar code number and the second-highest bar code number is 289,630,738. [6,810,008,421 - 6,520,377,683 = 289,630,738] Two hundred eighty-nine million, six hundred thirty thousand, seven hundred thirty-eight.

4. The sum of the two lowest bar code numbers is 7,594,483,270. [1,556,117,426 + 6,038,365,844 = 7,594,483,270] Seven billions, five hundred millions, nine ten millions, four hundred thousands, eight ten thousands, three thousands, two hundreds, seven tens, zero ones.

5. The difference between my answer in question 3 and my answer in question 2 is 4,964,260,257. [5,253,890,995 - 289,630,738 = 4,964,260,257]

6. The bar code sum for the left-hand set of numbers is 271,476. [15,561 + 60,383 + 62,229 + 65,203 + 68,100 = 271,476]

7. The average for the left-hand set of numbers only is 54,295. [271,476 (sum of left-hand numbers) / 5 (numbers) = 54,295 (rounded up from 54,295.2)] The closest number to this average is 60,383. [54,295 (average) - 15,561 (closest low number) = 38,734. 60,383 (closest high number) - 54,295 = 6088. 6088<38,734] The furthest number from this average is 15,561. [68,100 (highest number) - 54,295 (average) = 13,805. 54,295 (average) - 15,561 (lowest number) = 38,734. 38,734>13,805]

8. The bar code sum for the right-hand set of numbers is 170,378. [17,426 + 65,844 + 1004 + 77,683 + 8421 = 170,378]

9. The average for the right-hand set of numbers is 34,076. [170,378 (sum of right-hand numbers) / 5 (numbers) = 34,076 (rounded up from 34,075.6)] The closest number to this average is 17,426. [34,076 (average) - 17,426 (closest low number) = 16,650. 65,844 (closest high number) - 34,076 (average) = 31,768. 16,650<31,768] The farthest number from this average is 77,683. [77,683 (highest number) - 34,076 (average) = 43,607. 34,076 (average) - 1004 (lowest number) = 33,072. 43,607>33,072]

10. The difference between the higher (right-hand) bar code total and the lower (left-hand) bar code total is 101,098. [271,476 (left-hand total) - 170,378 (right-hand total) = 101,098]

Activity 64

Recipes for Fun

Look at the recipe for your favorite cooked food or baked good.

1. How many ingredients are listed in the recipe?
2. How many cups of ingredients do you need in total? How many tablespoons? How many teaspoons?
3. What is the most plentiful ingredient? What is the least plentiful ingredient?
4. How many dry ingredients does your recipe call for? How many wet ingredients?
5. What is the ratio of dry to wet ingredients? What is the ratio of wet to dry ingredients?
6. How many steps are shown?
7. What is the cooking or baking time?
8. What is the oven temperature?
9. How many people does the recipe serve or how much food does the recipe make?
10. Double the recipe and rewrite the ingredients list accordingly.

Answer Key

1. There are six (6) ingredients listed in the recipe.
2. I need $1\frac{3}{4}$ cups in total. [$\frac{1}{2} + \frac{1}{2} + \frac{1}{4} + \frac{1}{2} = \frac{2}{4} + \frac{2}{4} + \frac{1}{4} + \frac{2}{4} = \frac{7}{4} = 1\frac{3}{4}$.] I need 0 tablespoons. I need 1 teaspoon.
3. The most plentiful ingredient is apples, of which I need five (5). The least plentiful ingredient is ground cinnamon. I need one (1) tsp. of ground cinnamon.
4. My recipe calls for four (4) dry ingredients and two (2) wet ingredients.
5. The ratio of dry to wet ingredients is 2:1. [4:2. $4/2=2$. $2/2=1$. 2:1]
   The ratio of wet to dry ingredients is 1:2. [2:4. $2/2=1$. $4/2=2$. 1:2]
6. There are 11 steps shown.
7. The baking time is 45-50 minutes (or until apples are tender and topping is golden).
8. The oven temperature is 375°F (190°C).
9. The recipe yields four (4) servings. (In reality, it provides our family of five with one evening's worth of dessert.)
10. If I doubled the recipe, the rewritten ingredient list would be: 10 apples [5 apples x 2 = 10 apples], 1 cup firmly packed brown sugar [$\frac{1}{2}$ cup x $2 = \frac{1}{2} \times \frac{2}{1} = \frac{2}{2} = 1$ cup], 2 tsp ground cinnamon [1 tsp x 2 = 2 tsp], 1 cup all-purpose flour [$\frac{1}{2}$ cup x $2 = \frac{1}{2} \times \frac{2}{1} = \frac{2}{2} = 1$ cup], $\frac{1}{2}$ cup margarine [$\frac{1}{4}$ cup x $2 = \frac{1}{4} \times \frac{2}{1} = \frac{2}{4} = \frac{1}{2}$ cup], 1 cup quick-cooking rolled oats [$\frac{1}{2}$ cup x $2 = \frac{1}{2} \times \frac{2}{1} = \frac{2}{2} = 1$ cup].

Activity 65

Numbers, Numbers, Numbers, Everywhere

What to take: pen/pencil, piece of paper, digital watch, timer or watch with second hand

Where to go: your bedroom

What to do: Begin timing yourself as you walk into your bedroom. Look for five numbered objects.

1. How many seconds did it take you to find five objects with numbers on them? What were the objects?
2. On average, how long did it take you to find each object?
3. Write down the numbers printed on the five objects in the order you spotted them.
4. Rewrite your list and put the numbers in descending order.
5. What is the highest number on your list? What is the lowest number on your list? What is the difference between the highest and lowest numbers on your list?
6. What is the sum of the numbers on your list?
7. What is the mean of the numbers on your list?
8. What is the median number on your list?
9. What is the difference between the mean and the median?
10. Multiply the mean and median together. What is the product?

Answer Key

1. It took me 15 seconds to find five objects with numbers on them. The objects were: a prescription bottle; a travel itinerary; an antique thimble replica; a box of Christmas light bulbs; and a sample packet of body wash.
2. On average, it took me three (3) seconds to find each object. [15 seconds total time / 5 items = 3 seconds]
3. In the order I spotted them, the numbers are: 146,520; 82,000; 1552; 1200; 25.
4. The numbers in ascending order are: 25; 1200; 1552; 82,000; 146,520.
5. The highest number on my list is 146,520. The lowest number on my list is 25. The difference between the highest and lowest numbers on my list is 146,519.75. [146,520 - .25 = 146,519.75]
6. The sum of the numbers on my list is 231,272.25. [146,520 + 82,000 + 1552 + 200 + .25 = 231,272.25]
7. The mean of the numbers on my list is 45,254.45. [231,272.25 sum of numbers on list / 5 numbers on list = 46,254.45]
8. The median number on my list is 1552. [146,520; 82,000; 1552; 1200; .25]
9. The difference between the mean and the median is 44,702.45. [46,254.45 - 1552 = 44,702.45]
10. Multiplying the mean and median together yields a product of 71,786,906. [46,254.45 × 1552 = 71,786,906]

Magazine Mania

Pick up a magazine.

1. How many pages is the magazine, including front and back covers?

2. Turn the pages of the magazine and scan the type. Excluding the page numbers and running date folios, how many pages have numbers on them?

3. What percentage of the pages have a number on it?

4. Choose five pages at random. How many numbers appear on each page (excluding the pages number and running date folios)?

5. What is the average number of numbers that appear on the five pages in question 4? What is the mean number of numbers?

6. Express the magazine's bar code as a numeral. What is this number in words?

7. What is the ISSN number of the magazine? (Look in the magazine's masthead for the International Standard Serial Number.) Express this number in words.

8. What is the larger number, the bar code number or the ISSN number? What is the difference between the two numbers?

9. What is the newstand price of the magazine? What is the magazine's annual subscription rate? How many issues of the magazine are published each year? How much money would you save by subscribing to the magazine over buying each issue at the newstand?

10. Find three telephone numbers in the magazine. Express each phone number as a numeral. Add the three telephone numerals together. What is the sum?

Answer Key

1. Including front and back covers, the magazine is 136 pages. [132 inside pages + 4 pages front/back covers = 136]

2. There are numbers on 126 pages of the magazine.

3. Ninety-three (93) percent of the pages have numbers on them. [126 pages with numbers / 136 pages total × 100 = 92.6 = 93%]

4. There are 32, 16, 13, 5 and 6 numbers on the five pages.

5. There is an average of 14 numbers per page over the five pages. [32 + 16 + 13 + 5 + 6 = 72. 72 numbers / 5 pages = 14.4 = 14 pages] The mean number of numbers on the five pages is 13. [32, 16, 13, 6, 5]

6. The bar code number of the magazine is 7,098,910,227. In words, 7,098,910,227 is seven billion, ninety-eight million, nine hundred ten thousand, two hundred twenty-seven.

7. The ISSN number of the magazine is 0093-7673. Expressed as a numeral, this number is 937,673. In words, 937,673 is nine hundred thirty-seven thousand, six hundred seventy-three.

8. The bar code number is higher than the ISSN number. The difference between the two numbers is 7,097,972,554. [7,098,910,227 - 937,673 = 7,097,972,554]

9. The newstand price of the magazine is $2.99. The annual subscription rate is $103.48. There are 51 issues per year. [51 issues/year × $2.99/issue newstand price = $152.49/year newstand price. $152.49 newstand price - $103.48/year subscription rate = $49.01] I would save $49.01 by subscribing to the magazine rather than purchasing each issue at the newstand.

10. Answers will vary.

Food for Thought

1. How many food items are in the freezer in your refrigerator?
2. How many freezer items are fruits or vegetables in your freezer? What percentage of the food items in your freezer are fruits or vegetables?
3. How many freezer items are meat or fish? What percentage of the food items in your freezer are meat or fish?
4. How many freezer items are breads or pastries? What percentage of the food items in your freezer are breads or pastries?
5. How many freezer items are snacks or treats? What percentage of the food items in your freezer are snacks or treats?
6. List the contents of your freezer by category from least to most abundant. Which category has the most items in it? Which category has the least items in it? How many more food items are in the most popular category than in the least popular category?
7. If you had twice as many fruits or vegetables, three times as many meats or fish, four times as many breads or pastries and five times as many snacks or treats in your freezer as you did in question 6, how many food items would you have in your freezer?
8. If you had 1/5 as many snack or treats, 1/4 as many breads or pastries, 1/3 as many meats or fish and 1/2 as many fruits or vegetables in your freezer as you did in question 6, how many food items would you have in your freezer?
9. If you served one of each item to each of your family members at each meal (and assuming there was enough of the item to feed your whole family and that the item was completely consumed in one meal), for how many meals would the foods in each category last?
10. Choose two vegetable, two meat or fish, two bread or pastry and two snack/treat items found in your freezer. Choosing one item from each category, how many possible meal combinations can you create?

Answer Key

1. There are 36 food items in the freezer in my refrigerator.
2. Eleven (11) of the freezer items are fruits or vegetables. Thirty-one (31) percent of the food items in my freezer are fruits/vegetables. $[11 / 36 \times 100 = 30.5 = 31\%]$
3. Fifteen (15) of the freezer items are meat or fish. Forty-two (42) percent of the food items in my freezer are meat/fish. $[15 / 36 \times 100 = 41.6 = 42\%]$
4. Four (4) of the items in my freezer are breads or pastries. Eleven (11) percent of the food items in my freezer are breads/pastries. $[4 / 36 \times 100 = 11.1 = 11\%]$
5. Six (6) of the items in my freezer are snacks or treats. Seventeen (17) percent of the food items in my freezer are snacks/treats. $[6 / 36 \times 100 = 16.6 = 17\%]$
6. From least to most abundant the contents in my freezer are: meats/fish; fruits/vegetables; snacks/treats; breads/pastries. The meat/fish category has the most items in it. the breads/pastries category has the fewest items in it. There are 11 more of the most popular item than the least popular item. $[15 - 4 = 11]$
7. If I had twice as many fruits/vegetables, three times as many meats/fish, four times as many breads/pastries and five times as many snacks/treats in my freezer as I did in questions 2-5, I would have 113 food items in my freezer. $[11$ (fruits/vegetables) $\times 2 = 22.$ 15 (meats/fish) $\times 3 = 45.$ 4 (breads/pastries) $\times 4 = 16.$ 6 (snacks/treats) $\times 5 = 30.$ $22 + 45 + 16 + 30 = 113]$
8. If I had 1/5 as many snack/treats, 1/4 as many breads/pastries, 1/3 as many meats/fish and 1/2 as many fruits/vegetables in my freezer as I did in questions 2-5, I would have 13 food items in my freezer. $[6 \times 1/5 = 1.2 = 1.$ $4 \times 1/4 = 1.$ $15 \times 1/3 = 5.$ $11 \times 1/2 = 5.$ $5 = 6.$ $1 + 1 + 5 + 6 = 13]$
9. If I served one of each item to each of my family members at each meal, the fruits/vegetables would last for two (2) meals $[11$ fruits/vegetables / 5 family members $= 2.2 = 2$ meals], the meats/fish would last for three (3) meals $[15$ food items / 5 family members $= 3]$, the bread/pastries would last for less than one meal $[4$ food items / 5 family members $= 0.8]$, and the snack/treats would last for one (1) meal. $[6$ food items / 5 family members $= 1.2 = 1]$
10. If I chose frozen corn and frozen peas, ground beef and fish sticks, toaster danishes and a loaf of bread, and juice bars and frozen yogurt, I can create 16 possible meal combinations. $[4$ (one item from each category) $\times 4$ (categories) $= 16]$

Activity 68

Alphasorting

Ask a parent to buy a bag of alphabet pasta or a box of alphabet cereal.

1. Pour yourself a bowl of alphafood. Take a spoonful. How many letters are on your spoon? (You might want to transfer your spoonful to another bowl for alphasorting. Count only the complete or nearly complete letters.)
2. What letters are on your spoon?
3. Take two more spoonfuls of alphafood. How many letters are on each spoonful? (Make sure your spoonfuls are roughly the same size.)
4. What letters are on each spoonful?
5. On average, how many letters are on a spoonful of alphafood?
6. As you eat your bowl of alphafood, count each spoonful. How many spoonfuls were in your bowl of alphafood?
7. Approximately how many letters were in your bowl of alphafood?
8. What was the most common letter in your three spoonfuls of alphafood? How many of this letter did you find?
9. Based on your answer to question 8, approximately how many of the most common letter in your three spoonfuls of alphafood did your bowl contain?
10. Based on your answer to question 9, what percentage of the total number of letters in your bowl does the most popular letter account for?

Answer Key

1. There were 25 letters on my spoonful of alphapasta.
2. The following letters were on my spoon: f, f, o, o, o, o, r, a, w, u, i, i, z, l, q, q, q, b, v, v, s, e, j, p.
3. There are 23 and 29 letters respectively on my next two spoonfuls of alphapasta.
4. The following letters were on my second spoonful: r, r, b, b, k, y, x, n, f, m, m, v, v, v, j, j, t, t, p, p, s, q, q. The following letters were on my third spoonful: p, p, p, u, r, r, y, w, h, i, i, c, c, t, t, t, z, f, f, f, e, e, o, j, j, j, a, x, v. [25 + 23 + 29 = 77. 77 letters total / 3 spoonfuls = 25.6 = 26 letters.]
5. On average, there were 26 letters in a spoonful of alphapasta. [25 + 23 + 29 = 77. 77 letters total / 3 spoonfuls = 25.6 = 26 letters.]
6. There were 16 spoonfuls in my bowl of alphapasta.
7. There were approximately 416 letters in my bowl of alphapasta. [26 letters/spoonful x 16 spoonfuls/bowl = 416 letters/bowl]
8. The most common letter in my three spoonfuls of alphapasta was "v." I found seven (7) of this letter in my three spoonfuls. [f, f, f, f, f, o, o, o, o, o, r, r, r, r, a, w, u, u, i, i, i, i, z, z, l, q, q, q, q, q, v, v, v, v, v, v, v, s, s, e, e, j, j, j, j, j, b, b, b, k, y, y, x, x, n, m, m, t, t, t, t, p, p, p, p, p, h, c, c]
9. There were approximately 37 of the most common letter in my three spoonfuls of alphapasta in my bowl. [7 letters / 3 spoonfuls in trial = 2.3. 2.3 x 16 = 36.8 = 37]
10. The most popular letter in my three spoon trials, "v," accounts for approximately nine (9) percent of the total number of letters in my bowl. [37 "v"s/bowl / 416 letters/bowl x 100 = 8.9 = 9%]

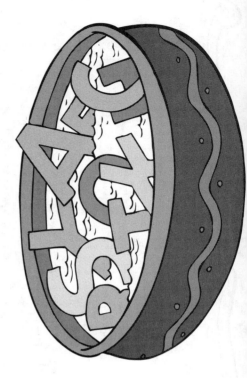

76

Activity 69

Digital Dishes

Count the number of dinner plates in your kitchen. (You will have to round down in this exercise to the nearest whole plate and meal!)

1. How many dinner-sized kitchen plates does your family possess?

2. How many are currently clean? How many are in the sink and/or dishwasher ready for washing? What is the ratio of clean to ready-for-washing plates?

3. How many different kinds (patterns and styles) of kitchen dinner plates do you have?

4. How many plates of each kind do you have? (Write your answer from least to most. Write a brief description of each kind of plate beside each number.)

5. What percentage of the total number of kitchen plates does your most popular kind of dinner plate represent?

6. If each person in your household used one plate at each meal, and assuming you threw away your dishes instead of washing them (wouldn't that be wasteful but fun!), after how many meals would you run out of plates?

7. Based on the assumptions in question 6, after how many meals would you run out of kitchen plates if you had 1½ times the number of plates?

8. Consider your average weekday and weekend meal patterns. How many plates does your household use every week? (Justify your answer.)

9. Based on your meal patterns in question 8, how many plates would you wash in a two-week period?

10. Based on your meal patterns in question 8, and assuming you wash the dishes every other evening, what is the minimum number of kitchen plates required to feed your family?

Finding an Outlet

Count, and only count, the number of electrical outlets in your home. __DO NOT TOUCH ANY ELECTRICAL OUTLET OR PLUG.__

1. How many electrical outlets are in your home?
2. How many rooms are in your home? (Count each hallway and foyer as a room.)
3. What is the average number of electrical outlets in each room?
4. If all of the receptacles were full of plugs, how many plugs would be plugged in?
5. If the circuit breakers blew on one-third of the outlets, how many available outlets would be left? How many plugs could be plugged in?
6. If half the outlets had two plugs plugged in and half the outlets had only one plug plugged in, how many plugs would be plugged in all together? (If there are an odd number of outlets in your home, eliminate one for this calculation.)
7. Based on averages, if each room had four times the number of outlets, how many plug receptacles would there be in total? If there were only half the number of outlets how many receptacles would there be in total?
8. If each outlet was fitted with one power bar (with five receptacles on each power bar) how many plugs could you plug in at once?
9. If only three plugs were plugged into each power bar, how many plugs would be plugged in? How many extra receptacles would be available?
10. Based on averages in question 3, if your home had three additional rooms, how many extra outlets would be available? How would this affect your outlet total in question 1? How many receptacles would be available in total?

Answer Key

1. There are 54 electrical outlets are in my home.
2. There are 18 rooms in my home.
3. The average number of electrical outlets in each room is 3. [54 outlets / 18 rooms = 3 outlets/room.]
4. If there was a plug in every available receptacle, 108 plugs would be plugged in. [54 outlets x 2 receptacles/outlet = 108 plugs]
5. If the circuit breakers blew 1/3 of the outlets, 36 plugs could still be plugged in. [54/1 x 1/3 = 18 outlets. 18 outlets x 2 receptacles/outlet = 36 plugs]
6. If half the outlet had two plugs and half of the outlets had only one plug, there would be 81 plugs plugged in. (54 outlets / 2 = 27. 27 x 2 = 54. 27 x 1 = 27. 54 + 27 = 81]
7. If each room had four times the number of outlets, there would be 432 receptacles in total. [3 outlets/room x 4 = 12 outlets/room. 12 outlets/room x 18 rooms = 216 outlets. 216 outlets x 2 receptacles/outlet = 432.] If there were only half the number of outlets, there would be 54 receptacles in total. [3 outlets/room x 1/2 = 1.5 outlets/room. 1.5 outlets/room x 18 rooms = 27 outlets. 27 outlets x 2 receptacles/outlet = 54 receptacles]
8. If each outlet was fitted with one power bar (with five receptacles on each power bar), 324 plugs could be plugged in. [54 outlets x 5 (receptacles/power bar) + 54 free receptacles = 324 receptacles]
9. If three plugs were plugged into each power bar, there would be 162 plugs plugged in. [54 outlets x 3 receptacles/outlet = 162 plugs] There would be 162 receptacles available. [324 available receptacles - 162 receptacles used = 162 extra receptacles available]
10. If my home had three additional rooms, there would be 9 additional outlets. This would increase my outlet total in question 1 by 9 from 54 to 63. I would have 18 new receptacles available. [9 x 2 = 18] and 126 receptacles in total. [108 + 18 = 126]

Activity 71

Bountiful Beds

Do a home bed count.

1. How many beds are in your home?

2. How many single, double, queen, king and bunk beds are in your home?

3. Assuming a single bed costs $350 to buy, a double costs $450, a queen costs $550, a king costs $650 and a set of bunk beds costs $500, how much money does your family have invested in beds?

4. Which type of bed is most common in your home? If you could sell all of these beds for half of their new furniture value in question 3, how much money could you raise?

5. What kind of bed (or beds), if any, could you buy with this money? (Justify your answer based on the new bed prices in question 3.)

6. How many people normally sleep in your home at night?

7. Assuming all the beds were full of sleeping bodies at night (ie. single = 1, double/queen/king/bunk = 2), how many people could sleep in your home?

8. Based on your answers in questions 6 & 7, how many unused bed spaces are normally available in your house at night?

9. If you were running your home like a hotel and could rent out your unused bed spaces according to the following fee schedule: single=$25, double=$30, queen=$35, king=$40, bunk=$25, how much rental income could you make (based on your answer in question 8) every night?

10. If your family went away for one week and rented out your household's total bed space every night, how much income could you generate? (Use the answer from question 2, the capacity schedule from question 7 and the fee schedule from question 9.)

Answer Key

1. There are 6 beds in my home.

2. There are four double beds, one queen-sized bed and one single bed in my home.

3. My family has $2600 invested in beds. [4 × $450 = $1800. 1 × 550 = $550. 1 × $350 = $350. $1800 + $550 + $350 = $2600]

4. The double bed is most common in my home. If I sold all of our double beds for half of their new furniture value in question 3, I could raise $900. [$1800 × ½ = $900]

5. I could buy two (2) new single beds. [$350 × 2 = $700.] I could buy two (2) new double beds. [$450 × 2 = $900] I could buy one (1) new single bed and one new double bed. [$350 + $450 = $800] I could buy one (1) new single bed and one (1) new queen bed. [$350 + $550 = $900] I could buy one new single bed and one new set of bunk beds. [$350 + $500 = $850] I could buy one (1) new king bed [$650.]

6. Five (5) people normally sleep in my home at night.

7. If all the beds in my home were full at night, we could accommodate 11 sleeping bodies. [4 double beds × 2 people/bed = 8 people. 1 queen bed × 2 people/bed = 2 people. 1 single bed × 1 person/bed = 1 person. 8 people + 2 people + 1 person = 11 people]

8. There are normally 6 unused bed spaces in our house at night. [11 available bed spaces - 5 sleeping people = 6 unused bed spaces]

9. We could make $180 by renting our leftover bed space every night. [There are normally 4 double bed spaces, 1 single bed space and 1 queen bed space available in our house at night. 4 × $30 = $120. 1 × $25 = $25. 1 × $35 = $35. $120 + $25 + $35 = $180]

10. If we went away for one week and fully rented out our bed space every night we were away, we could generate $2345. [4 double beds × 2 spaces/bed = 8 bed spaces × $30/bed space = $240. 1 queen bed × 2 spaces/bed × $35/bed space = $70. 1 single bed × 1 space/bed × $25/bed space = $25. $240 + $70 + $25 = $335/night × 7 nights = $2345/week]

Super Shoppers

Ask a parent if you can look at a recent receipt from a grocery store. (If possible, there should be at least 20 items on the receipt.)

1. What is the total amount on the cash register receipt? (Express this figure in numbers and in words.)
2. How many items are on the receipt?
3. What is the price of the most expensive item? What is the price of the least expensive item?
4. What is the average price of an item on this receipt?
5. List the prices of the first 10 items in order of expense, from least to most. What is the average of these 10 items? How does this compare to the average for the total bill?
6. List the prices of the last 10 items in order of expense, from most to least. What is the average of these 10 items? How does this compare to the average for the total bill?
7. What is the total tax on the bill?
8. What percentage of the bill does the tax account for?
9. For what percentage of the receipt do the three most expensive items account? If you subtract these items from the bill, what happens to the average price per item?
10. For what percentage of the receipt do the three least expensive items account? If you subtract these items from the bill, what happens to the average price per item?

Answer Key

1. The total amount on the cash register receipt is $109.55, or one hundred nine dollars and fifty-five cents.
2. There are 38 items on the receipt.
3. The price of the most expensive item is $9.99. The price of the least expensive item is $50.
4. The average price of an item on this receipt is $2.88. [$109.55 (receipt total) / 38 (items on receipt) = $2.88]
5. From least to most expensive, the prices of the first 10 items on the receipt are: $.67, $.99, $.99, $1.69, $1.99, $1.99, $1.99, $2.13, $2.14, $2.99. The average of these 10 items is $1.56, which is $1.32 less than the average for the entire bill. [17.57 (sum of items) / 10 (number of items) = 1.76 (rounded up from 1.757). $2.88 - $1.76 = $1.12]
6. From most to least expensive, the prices of the last 10 items on the receipt are: $9.99, $4.49, $4.19, $3.99, $1.19, $1.09, $.94, $.79, $.79. The average of these 10 items is $2.87, which is only one cent less than the average for the entire bill. [28.65 (sum of items) / 10 (number of items) = 2.87 (rounded up from 2.865). $2.88 - $2.87 = $.01]
7. The total tax on the bill is $4.54.
8. The tax accounts for four (4) percent of the total bill. [$4.54 (total tax) / $109.55 (receipt total) x 100 = 4% (rounded down from 4.14)]
9. The three most expensive items account for 24 percent of the total bill. If I subtract these items from the bill, the average price per item drops by 51 cents. [$9.99 + $9.99 + $6.74 = $26.72. $26.72 (sum of items) / $109.55 (total bill) x 100 = 24% (rounded down from 24.39).] $109.55 (total bill) - $26.72 (sum of items) = $82.83. $82.83 (new total) / 35 (items remaining on receipt) = $2.37 (rounded up from 2.366). $2.88 (average price/item) - $2.37 (new average price/item = $.51]
10. The three least expensive items account for 2 percent of the total bill. If I subtract these items from the bill, the average price per item increases by 19 cents. [$.50 + $.67 + $.79 = $1.96 (sum of items) / $109.55 (total bill) x 100 = 2% (rounded up from 1.789). $109.55 (total bill) - $1.96 (sum of items) = $107.59 (new total) / 35 (items remaining on bill) = $3.07. $3.07 (new average) - $2.88 (old average) = $.19]

Don't Count your Eggs Until They're Cooked

Pretend that you are going to make a lovely egg breakfast for your family. (You will have to find out the preferences of your family members—scrambled, boiled, poached, fried, over-easy, sunny-side up, omelette, etc.—to complete this activity.)

1. If everyone in your family (including you!) wanted two eggs, how many eggs would you have to cook?

2. If the adults wanted three eggs each and the kids (including you!) wanted two eggs each, how many eggs would you have to cook?

3. If your family had eggs for breakfast every Saturday and Sunday, how many eggs would you use in a month, based on the adult/kid egg numbers in question 2?

4. Using the adult/kid egg numbers from question 2, how many eggs would you have to cook if your next door neighbors joined your family for breakfast?

5. How do your family members prefer their eggs? (Record their preferences.)

6. If an omelette takes four eggs, scrambled eggs take three eggs, and the other cooking variations require a single egg each, how many eggs will your family use at breakfast (based on their preferences from question 5)?

7. If you need to add 1/4 cup of milk for an omelette and 1/2 cup of milk for scrambled eggs, and each family member has 1 cup of milk with his or her meal, how much milk will you use at breakfast?

8. Using the information from question 6, and assuming that your family has eggs for breakfast every Saturday, how many eggs will your family devour in one year?

9. How many people would like toast with their eggs? How many people would like bacon, ham or sausages? How many of each side order would they like with their eggs? How many pieces of toast, bacon, ham and sausages will you need to satisfy their appetites at one meal?

10. If you could have the egg of your choice and two side orders (including toast, bacon, ham and sausages), from how many possible meal combinations could you choose? What are the possible combinations?

Answer Key

1. If everyone in my family (including me!) wanted two eggs, I would have to cook 10 eggs. [5 family members x 2 eggs/family member = 10 eggs]

2. If the adults wanted three eggs each, and the kids wanted two eggs each, I would have to cook 12 eggs. [2 adults x 3 eggs = 6 eggs. 3 kids x 2 eggs = 6 eggs. 6 eggs + 6 eggs = 12 eggs]

3. If my family had eggs for breakfast every Saturday and Sunday, we would use 96 eggs in a month, based on the adult/kid egg numbers in question 2. [12 eggs/day x 2 days/week x 4 weeks/month = 96 eggs]

4. I would have to cook 24 eggs if our next door neighbors joined us for breakfast. [2 adults x 3 eggs = 6 eggs. 3 kids x 2 eggs = 6 eggs. 6 eggs + 6 eggs = 12 eggs. 12 eggs (our family) + 12 eggs (neighbor family) = 24 eggs]

5. I like my eggs over easy; Jonathan like his eggs sunny-side up; Matthew and Stephanie like their eggs scrambled; and Patrick likes his eggs in an omelette.

6. If an omelette takes four eggs, scrambled eggs take three eggs, and the other cooking variations require a single egg each, my family will use 12 eggs at breakfast based on their preferences from question 5. [1 omelette x 4 eggs = 4 eggs. 2 scrambled x 3 eggs = 6 eggs. 1 over easy x 1 egg = 1 egg. 1 sunny-side up x 1 egg = 1 egg. 4 eggs + 6 eggs + 1 egg + 1 egg = 12 eggs]

7. If I need to add 1/4 cup of milk for an omelette and 1/2 cup of milk for scrambled eggs, and each of my family member has 1 cup of milk with his or her meal, I will use 5 3/4 cups of milk at breakfast. [1 omelette x 1/4 cup milk = 1/4 cup milk. 2 scrambled x 1/2 cup milk = 1 cup milk. 5 family members x 1 cup milk = 5 cups milk. 1/4 + 1 + 5 = 6 1/4 cups milk]

8. Using the information from question 6, and assuming that my family has eggs for breakfast every Saturday, we will devour 624 eggs or 52 dozen eggs in one year. [12 eggs/Saturday x 52 Saturdays/year = 624 eggs/year] [625 eggs / 12 eggs/dozen = 52 dozen]

9. We would need 6 pieces of toast, 6 sausages, 2 pieces of ham and 20 slices of bacon to satisfy the appetites of my family at one meal. [Jonathan: 2 pieces toast and 4 sausages; Tracey: 1 piece toast and 2 pieces ham; Matthew: 1 piece toast and 8 pieces bacon; Patrick no toast and 12 pieces bacon; Stephanie 2 pieces toast and 2 sausages. 2 + 1 + 1 + 0 + 2 = 6 toast. 4 + 2 = 6 sausages. 2 ham. 8 + 12 = 20 bacon]

Activity 74

Eye Charts

Record the eye color of each student in your class.

1. How many brown-eyed children are in your class?
2. How many blue-eyed children are in your class?
3. How many gray/green/hazel-eyed children are in your class?
4. Which eye color is predominant? Which eye colour is the most rare? How many more children have eyes of the dominant colour than eyes of the other two color groups? Express these comparisons as ratios.
5. How many of your fellow students share your eye color?
6. For what percentage of the class total does your eye color account?
7. How would the balance change if you grouped blue and gray/green/hazel together?
8. Make a chart to show the eye color statistics in your class.
9. Ask a neighboring class to do this activity. How do the results from that class compare to yours? How do they differ?
10. When the eye-color statistics of the two classes are combined, what percentage of children in the two classes shares your eye color?

Word Leaders

According to The American Heritage Word Frequency Book, the word the represents 7.3% of all words used in school texts. The word of represents 2.9% of all words used in school texts. These two words make up more than 10% (10.2%) of the words used in our school books! The words and, a, to, is and on represent another 9.9% (2.6%, 2.5%, 2.4%, 1.2% and 1.2% respectively) of the words we read in school every day!

1. Choose a school text. Open the book to a full page of text. Count the number of words on the page. How many words are on the page?

2. Based on the Word Frequency Book's declaration, how many times should the word the appear on the page?

3. Based on the Word Frequency Book's declaration, how many times should the word of appear on the page?

4. Based on the Word Frequency Book's declaration, how many times should the word group and, a, to, is and on appear on the page?

5. See if the word frequency rule holds true. Count the number of the's on the page. Count the number of of's on the page. Count and combine in a single group the number of and's, a's, to's, is's and on's on the page. How many times did each appear on the page?

6. Were the Word Frequency Book predictions accurate? If not, by how much were they off?

7. How many pages are in the book?

8. Based on the Word Frequency Book's predictions, how many times should the words the and of appear in the book?

9. Based on the Word Frequency Book's predictions, how many times should the word group and, a, to, is and on appear in the book?

10. Based on your predictions, how many times should the words and and the and the word group and, a, to, is and on appear in the book?

Answer Key

I used a novel for this activity to see if the rules hold true for "trade" publications as well as educational works.

1. There are 377 words on the page.

2. Based on the Word Frequency Book's declaration, the word the should appear on the page 28 times. [377 x .073 = 27.5 = 28]

3. Based on the Word Frequency Book's declaration, the word of should appear on the page 11 times. [377 x .029 = 10.9 = 11]

4. Based on the Word Frequency Book's declaration, the word group and, a, to, is and on should appear on the page 37 times. [377 x .099 = 37.3 = 37]

5. The word the appeared on the page 11 times. The word of appeared on the page four (4) times. The word group and (9), a (13), to (9), is (1) and on (2) appeared on the page times 34 times. [9 + 13 + 9 + 1 + 2 = 34]

6. The Word Frequency Book prediction for the word the was not accurate. The word the appeared 17 times less frequently than predicted. [28 - 11 = 17] The Word Frequency Book prediction for the word of was not accurate. The word of appeared seven (7) times less frequently than predicted. [11 - 4 = 7.] The Word Frequency Book prediction for the word group and, a, to, is and on was fairly accurate. The word group and, a, to, is and on appeared three (3) times less frequently than predicted. [37 - 34 = 3]

7. There are 535 pages in the book.

8. Based on the Word Frequency Book's predictions, the words the and on should appear in the book 14,980 and 5885 times respectively. [The: 28 x 535 = 14,980. Of: 11 x 535 = 5885]

9. Based on the Word Frequency Book's predictions, the word group and, a, to, is and on should appear in the book 19,795 times. [37 x 535 = 19,795]

10. Based on my predictions, the word the should appear in the book 5885 times [11 x 535 = 5885], the word of should appear in the book 2140 times [4 x 535 = 2140] and the word group and, a, to, is and on should appear in the book 18,190 times. [34 x 535 = 18,190]

School Timing

1. On an average day, how much time do you spend at school? (To calculate: measure from the time you set foot on school property in the morning to the time you step off school property in the afternoon.) Express your answer in hours and minutes.

2. How much time do you spend at recess? (Include before- and after-school time.)

3. How much time do you spend at lunch?

4. How much time do you spend doing extra-curricular activities?

5. How much time each day do you spend in actual studies?

6. In a week, how much time do you spend in actual studies?

7. How much time do you spend at lunch and recess in one week?

8. How much time do you spend in actual studies over the course of a month?

9. How much time do you spend at lunch and recess over the course of a month?

10. How much time do you spend in actual studies over the course of the school year? (Make sure you take holidays into account in your calculation!)

Answer Key

1. On an average day, my sons are on school property from 8:20 a.m. to 4:00 p.m. They spend 8 hours, 40 minutes (or 520 minutes) [8:20 a.m. - 4:00 p.m.] at school. [8 hours x 60 minutes/hour = 480 + 40 minutes = 520 minutes]

2. They spend 1 hour, 15 minutes (or 75 minutes) at recess.

3. They spend 1 hour (or 60 minutes) at lunch.

4. They spend 10 minutes doing extra-curricular activities.

5. They spend 6 hours, 15 minutes (or 375 minutes) each day doing actual studies. [520 (total time at school) - 75 (recess) - 60 (lunch) - 10 (extra curricular) = 375 minutes. 375 minutes / 60 minutes/hour = 6.25. 6 hours with 0.25 hours remainder. 0.25 x 60 minutes/hour = 15 minutes. 6 hours, 15 minutes]

6. In a week, my sons spend 31 hours, 15 minutes (or 1875 minutes) in actual studies. [375 minutes/day x 5 days/week = 1875 minutes/week. 1875 minutes / 60 minutes/hour = 31.25. 31 hours, 15 minutes]

7. They spend 11 hours, 15 minutes (or 675 minutes) at lunch and recess in one week. [60 minutes/day (lunch) x 5 days/week = 300 minutes lunch. 75 minutes/day (recess) x 5 days/week = 375 minutes recess. 300 + 375 = 675 minutes. 675 minutes / 60 minutes/hour = 11.25. 11 hours, 15 minutes]

8. They spend 125 hours (or 7500 minutes) in actual studies over the course of a month. [1875 minutes/week x 4 weeks/month = 7500 minutes/month. 7500 minutes / 60 minutes/hour = 125 hours/month]

9. They spend 45 hours (or 2700 minutes) at lunch and recess over the course of a month. [675 minutes/week x 4 weeks/month = 2700 minutes/month. 2700 / 60 = 45 hours/month]

10. They spend 1125 hours (or 67,500 minutes) in actual studies over the course of the school year. [7500 minutes/month x 9 months/year = 67,500 minutes/year. 67,500 minutes/year / 60 minutes/hour = 1125 hours/year]

MATH

SCIENCE

LANGUAGE

SOCIAL STUDIES

PHYSICAL EDUCATION

ART

MUSIC

SPANISH

Activity 77

Study Hour

Look at your timetable or study schedule and determine:

1. How many hours each week/month do you spend learning math at school?

2. How many hours each week/month do you spend learning science at school?

3. How many hours each week/month do you spend learning language arts at school?

4. How many hours each week/month do you spend learning social studies at school?

5. How many hours each week/month do you spend learning physical education at school?

6. How many hours each week/month do you spend learning music at school?

7. How many hours each week/month do you spend learning a second language at school?

8. How many hours each week/month do you spend learning visual arts at school?

9. What subject you spend the most hours learning each week? What subject you spend the least hours learning each week? What is the difference between the most and least studied subjects?

10. What percentage of your total study time you spend learning the subject that receives most teaching time? What percentage of your total study time do you spend learning the subject that receives the least teaching time.

Answer Key

1. My son, Patrick, spends 6 hours, 40 minutes each week and 26 hours, 40 minutes each month learning math at school. [WEEK: 80 minutes/day x 5 day/week = 400 minutes/week. 400 / 60 minutes/hour = 6.67. 6 hours with 0.67 hours remainder: 0.67 x 60 minutes/hour = 40.2 = 40 minutes. 6 hours, 40 minutes. MONTH: 400 minutes/week x 4 weeks/month = 1600 minutes/month. 1600 minutes/month / 60 minutes/hour = 26.67. 26 hours with 0.67 hours remainder: 0.67 x 60 minutes/hour = 40.2 = 40 minutes. 26 hours, 40 minutes.]

2. My son, Patrick, spends 2 hours, 40 minutes each week and 10 hours, 40 minutes each month learning science at school. [WEEK: 40 minutes/day x 4 days/week = 160 minutes/week. 160 / 60 = 2.67. 2 hours with 0.67 hours remainder: 0.67 x 60 = 40.2 = 40 minutes. MONTH: 160 minutes/week x 4 weeks/month = 640 minutes/month. 640 / 60 = 10.67. 10 hours with 0.67 hours remainder, or 40 minutes.]

3. My son, Patrick, spends 7 hours, 20 minutes each week and 29 hours, 20 minutes each month learning language arts at school. [WEEK: 80 minutes/day x 4 days/week = 320. 120 minutes/day x 1 day/week = 120. 320 + 120 = 440 minutes/week. 440 / 60 = 7.33. 7 hours with 0.33 hours remainder. 0.33 x 60 = 19.8 = 20. 7 hours, 20 minutes. MONTH: 440 minutes/week x 4 weeks/month = 1760. 1760 minutes / 60 minutes/hour = 29.33. 29 hours with 0.33 hours remainder, or 20 minutes.]

4. My son, Patrick, spends 2 hours each week and 8 hours each month learning social studies at school. [WEEK: 40 minutes/day x 3 days/week = 120 minutes/week. 120 minutes/week x 4 weeks/month = 480 minutes/month. MONTH: 120 minutes/week x 4 weeks/month = 480 minutes/month. 480 minutes/month / 60 minutes/hour = 8 hours.]

5. My son, Patrick, spends 2 hours each week and 8 hours each month learning physical education at school. [WEEK: 40 minutes/day x 3 days/week = 120 minutes/week. 120 minutes/week x 4 weeks/month = 480 minutes/month. MONTH: 120 minutes/week x 4 weeks/month = 480 minutes/month. 480 minutes/month / 60 minutes/hour = 8 hours.]

6. My son, Patrick, spends 1 hour, 20 minutes each week and 5 hours, 20 minutes each month learning music at school. [WEEK: 40 minutes/day x 2 days/week = 80 minutes/week. 80 minutes / 60 minutes/hour = 1.33. 1 hour with 0.33 hours remainder: 0.33 x 60 minutes/hour = 19.8 = 20. 1 hour, 20 minutes. MONTH: 80 minutes/week x 4 weeks/month = 320 minutes/month. 320 minutes / 60 minutes/hour = 5.33. 5 hours with 0.33 hours remainder. 0.33 minutes x 60 minutes/hour = 19.8 = 20. 5 hours, 20 minutes.]

7. My son, Patrick, spends 3 hours, 20 minutes each week and 13 hours, 20 minutes each month learning a second language at school. [WEEK: 40 minutes/day x 5 days/week = 200 minutes/week. 200 minutes / 60 minutes/hour = 3.33. 3 hours, 20 minutes. MONTH: 200 minutes/week x 4 weeks/month = 800 minutes/month. 800 minutes / 60 minutes/hour = 13.3. 13 hours, 20 minutes.]

8. My son, Patrick, spends 1 hour, 20 minutes each week and 5 hours, 20 minutes each month learning visual arts at school. [WEEK: 80 minutes/day x 1 day/week = 80 minutes/week. 80 minutes / 60 minutes/hour = 1.33. 1 hour with 0.33 hours remainder: 0.33 x 60 minutes/hour = 19.8 = 20. 1 hour, 20 minutes. MONTH: 80 minutes/week x 4 weeks/month = 320 minutes/month. 320 minutes / 60 minutes/hour = 5.33. 5 hours with 0.33 hours remainder. 0.33 minutes x 60 minutes/hour = 19.8 = 20. 5 hours, 20 minutes.]

9. My son, Patrick, spends the most hours learning language arts each week. He spends the least hours learning music and visual arts each week. Patrick spends six (6) hours more each week learning language arts than music and six (6) hours more each week learning language arts than visual arts. [440 minutes (language arts) - 80 minutes (music and visual arts) = 360 minutes. 360 minutes / 60 minutes/hour = 6 hours.]

10. Patrick spends 28 percent of his total study time each week studying language arts, 5 percent of his total study time each week studying music and 5 percent of his total study time each week studying visual arts. [400 + 160 + 440 + 120 + 120 + 80 + 200 + 80 = 1600 minutes total study time/week. 440 minutes (language arts) / 1600 minutes (total) x 100 = 27.5 = 28%. 80 minutes (music and visual arts) / 1600 minutes (total) x 100 = 5%.]

Activity 78

For the Love of Heights

Record the height of each student in your class.

1. What is the tallest recorded height?
2. What is the shortest recorded height?
3. What is the combined height of the students in your class?
4. What is the mean height of the students in your class?
5. Arrange the students according to height from tallest to shortest.
6. What is the median (middle) recorded height of the students in your class?
7. How tall are you? How does your height compare to the tallest recorded height? How does your height compare to the shortest recorded height?
8. How does your height compare to the mean height of the students in your class? How does your height compare to the median height of the students in your class?
9. Draw a class height graph with Height on the vertical axis and Student's Name on the horizontal axis. (Arrange the student names according to height so that your height graph ascends from left to right or descends from left to right.)
10. Ask a neighboring class to complete this activity. Repeat the activity comparing data from the neighboring class to your personal height statistic.

Answer Key

1. The tallest recorded height in my son's class is 5' 9".
2. The shortest recorded height in Matthew's class is 4'10".
3. The combined height of the students in Matthew's class is 93'3".
   [5'9" + 5'7" + 5'4" + 5'4" + 5'3" + 5'2" + 5'2" + 5'2" + 5'2" +
   5'1" + 5'1" + 5'1" + 5'1" + 5' + 5' + 4'11" + 4'10" = 88' 63". 63" /
   12"/foot = 5.25. 5' with 0.25 foot remainder. 0.25 x 12 inches/foot =
   3". 88' + 5' = 93' 3"]
4. The mean height of the students in Matthew's class is 4'9". [93 feet
   x 12 inches/foot = 1116 + 3 = 1119 inches. 1119 inches total height / 18
   students = 62.17 = 62 inches. 62 inches / 12 inches/foot = 5.2.
   5 feet with 0.2 foot remainder. 0.2 x 12 inches/foot = 2.4 = 2 inches.
5. Arranged according to height from tallest to shortest, the students
   in Matthew's class are: [5'9" (Zack), 5'7" (Caleb), 5'4" (Chris), 5'4"
   (Tyler), 5'3" (Rob), 5'3" (Mike), 5'2" (Matt), 5'2" (Jeff), 5'2" (Rebecca),
   5'2" (Natalie), 5'1" (Alexandra), 5'1" (Alex), 5'1" (Kelley), 5'1" (Sarah), 5'
   (Ty), 5' (Adam), 4'11" (Caitlin), 4'10" (James)]
6. The median (middle) recorded height of the students in Matthew's
   class is 5'2". [5'9", 5'7", 5'4", 5'4", 5'3", 5'3", 5'2", 5'2", 5'2", 5'1",
   5'1", 5'1", 5', 5', 4'11", 4'10"]
7. Matthew is 5'2" tall. He is 7" inches shorter than the tallest person
   in his class. [5'9" - 5'2" = 7"] He is 4" inches taller than the shortest
   person in his class. [5'2" = 5 x 12 = 60 + 2 = 62". 4'10" = 4 x 12 =
   48 + 10 = 58. 62" - 58" = 4"]
8. Matthew is the same height, 5'2", as the average height of a student
   in his class. [62" = 62"] Matthew is the same height, 5'2", as the
   median height of the students in his class. [5'2" =5'2"]

Activity 79

The Birthday Club

Record the birthdate (dd/mm/yy) of each of your classmates.

1. Make a chart to show how many of your classmates were born in each month.

2. Make a chart to show how many of your classmates were born on each date of the month.

3. In what month were you born? How many of your classmates share your birth month? What percent of students in your class were born in this month?

4. On what date of the month were you born? How many of your classmates were born on the same date of the month as you? What percent of students in your class were born on this date?

5. What is (are) the most popular birth month(s)? How many births occur in this (these) month(s)? What percent of your classmates were born in the most popular birth month(s)?

6. What is (are) the most popular birthdate(s)? How many students were born on the most popular birthdate(s)? What percent of your classmates were born on the most popular birthdate(s)?

7. Express each birthdate as a numeral. Arrange the birthdates in numerical order from largest to smallest. Add the birthdates together. What is the sum?

8. Subtract your birthdate from the sum in question 7. What is the difference?

9. Divide the sum of the birthdates in question 7 by the number of kids in your class. What is the quotient?

10. Make two graphs, one to show birth months (with Number of Students on the vertical axis and Birth Month on the horizontal axis) and one to show birthdays (with Number of Students on the vertical axis and Day of the Month on the horizontal axis).

Answer Key

1. January-0, February-1, March-2, April-0, May-4, June-2, July-0, August-2, September-4, October-1, November-0, December-2

2. 1-1, 8-1, 9-1, 12-2, 15-1, 17-1, 18-2, 19-1, 21-3, 22-1, 24-1, 25-1, 7-1, 29-1

3. Matthew was born in August. Only one other student in his class was born in August. Eleven (11) percent of students in Matthew's class were born in August. [2 students / 18 students total x 100 = 11.1 = 11%]

4. Matthew was born on the 12th. Only one other student in his class was born on the 12th. Eleven (11) percent of students in your class share his birthdate. [2 students / 18 students total x 100 = 11.1 = 11%]

5. September and May are the most popular birth months with four (4) births. Twenty-two percent of Matthew's classmates were born in the most popular birth months. [4 births / 18 births total x 100 = 22.2 = 22%]

6. The most popular birthdate is the 21st. Three kids were born on the 21st. Seventeen percent of Matthew's classmates were born on the most popular birthdate. [3 births / 18 births total x 100 = 16.7 = 17%]

7. Expressed in numerical form and arranged from largest to smallest the birthday list reads: 121,288; 120,987; 102,987; 92,587; 92,188; 92,187; 90,888; 81, 888; 81,287; 62,488; 61,787; 52,187; 51,987; 51,588; 50,188; 32, 788; 31,887; 22,288. Adding the birthdates together yields a sum of 1,293,475. [121,288 + 120,987 + 102,987 + 92,587 + 92,188 + 92,187 + 90,888 + 81, 888 + 81,287 + 62,488 + 61,787 + 52,187 + 51,987 + 51,588 + 50,188 + 32, 788 + 31,887 + 22,288 = 1,293,475]

8. Subtracting Matthew's birthdate from the sum in question 7 yields a difference of 1,212,188. [1,293,475 - 81,287 = 1,212,188]

9. Dividing the sum of the birthdates in question 7 by the number of kids in Matthew's class yields a product of 71,860. [1,293,475 birthdate total / 18 kids in class = 71,859.7 = 71,860]

Activity 80

Class Dribble Challenge

For this activity you will need a basketball, a piece of paper, a pencil or pen, a clock or watch, and all the kids in your class!

At recess or during gym, have the students in your class take turns dribbling a basketball. Time each "dribbler" for one minute. See how many times the dribbler can bounce the ball in the one-minute time period. Count each bounce out loud as a class. A dribbler's turn continues until the minute expires. (In the event of a mid-turn fumble, the dribbler should recover the ball as quickly as possible and continue bouncing.) Record each dribbler's bounce total on the piece of paper.

1. What is your dribble count?
2. How does your dribble count compare to the highest dribble count?
3. How does your dribble count compare to the lowest dribble count?
4. What is your class's total dribble count?
5. For what percent of the class dribble total does your dribble total account?
6. What is the median (middle score) of the class's individual dribble counts? What is the mode of the class's individual dribble counts (the score that occurs most frequently)?
7. What is the class dribble average?
8. What is the difference between your dribble count and the class dribble average?
9. Express your dribble count as a fraction of the class average.
10. Eliminate the highest and lowest dribble counts from the class total. How does this affect the class average?

Answer Key

1. My son Patrick's dribble count was 134.
2. Patrick's dribble count of 134 was 8 less than the highest dribble count of 142. [142 - 134 = 8]
3. Patrick's dribble count of 134 was 54 more than the lowest dribble count of 80. [134 - 80 = 54]
4. The class dribble count total was 2974. [103 + 142 + 110 + 80 + 110 + 102 + 110 + 138 + 121 + 130 + 127 + 111 + 112 + 121 + 98 + 103 + 120 + 95 + 110 + 134 + 85 + 110 + 122 + 100 + 140 + 140 = 2974]
5. Patrick's dribble count average accounts for five (5) percent of the class dribble total. [134 (Patrick) / 2974 (class) × 100 = 4.5 = 5%]
6. The median (middle score) of the class's individual dribble counts is 111. [142 + 140 + 140 + 138 + 134 + 130 + 127 + 122 + 121 + 121 + 120 + 112 + 111 + 110 + 110 + 110 + 103 + 103 + 102 + 100 + 100 + 98 + 95 + 85 + 80. 111 + 110 = 221. 221 / 2 = 110.5 =111] The mode of the class's individual dribble counts is 110. [110 occurs four times. 110 occurs more times than any other number]
7. The class dribble count average is 114. [2974 total dribbles / 26 kids in class = 114.4 = 114 dribble average]
8. Patrick's dribble count of 134 is 20 dribbles higher than the class dribble average of 114. [134 (Patrick) - 114 = 20]
9. Patrick's dribble count, expressed as a fraction of the class average is 67/57. [134/114. 67/57]
10. When the highest and lowest dribble counts are eliminated from the class total, the class dribble average increases by one (1) from 114 to 115. [2974 - 142 - 80 = 2752. 2752 new class total / 24 kids remaining = 114.7 = 115. 115 - 114 = 1]

Kids in the Hall

1. Estimate how many steps it will take you to get to the nearest water fountain from the doorway of your classroom.
2. Make the journey. How many steps did it take you?
3. What is the difference between your estimate and the actual trip distance?
4. Estimate how many steps it will take you to get to the office from the nearest water fountain.
5. Make the journey. How many steps did it take you?
6. What is the difference between your estimate and the actual trip distance?
7. Estimate how many steps it will take you to get to the gymnasium from the office.
8. Make the journey. How many steps did it take you?
9. What is the difference between your estimate and the actual trip distance?
10. How many trips did you overestimate? How many trips did you underestimate?

Answer Key

Since I do not spend my days in school, I will estimate distances in my home.

1. I estimate that it will take me 33 steps to get to the kitchen sink from my office desk.
2. I made the journey and it actually took me 29 steps to get to the kitchen sink from my office desk.
3. The difference between my estimate and the actual trip distance was four (4) steps. [33 steps (estimate) - 29 steps (actual distance) = 4 steps]
4. I estimate that it will take me 28 steps to get from the kitchen sink to the front door.
5. I made the journey and it actually took me 23 steps to get from the kitchen sink to the front door.
6. The difference between my estimate and the actual trip distance was five (5) steps. [28 steps (estimate) - 23 steps (actual distance) = 5 steps]
7. I estimate that it will take me 16 steps to get to the bathroom from the front door.
8. I made the journey and it actually took me 18 steps to get from the front door to the bathroom.
9. The difference between my estimate and the actual trip distance was two (2) steps. [18 steps (actual distance) - 16 steps (estimate) = 2 steps]
10. I overestimated two trips: the trip from my office desk to the kitchen sink and my trip from the kitchen sink to the front door. I underestimated one trip: my trip from the front door to the bathroom.

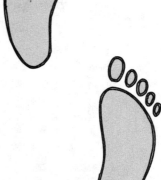

Activity 82

Pen 'n Pencil 'Parisons

Find out how many pens and pencils all of your classmates have in their desks.

1. How many pens are in your desk? How many pencils are in your desk?

2. Which of your classmates has the most pens? How many pens does he or she have? How does your pen total compare to this person's pen total?

3. Which of your classmates has the most pencils? How many pencils does he or she have? How does your pencil total compare to this person's pencil total?

4. How many pens do you and your classmates have in total?

5. For what percent of the class pen total does your pen collection account?

6. How many pencils do you and your classmates have in total?

7. For what percent of the class pencil total does your pencil collection account?

8. How many students are in your class? What is the average number of pens per person in your class? How does your pen collection compare to the class average?

9. What is the average number of pencils per person in your class? How does your pencil average compare to the class pencil average?

10. Add together the number of pens and pencils possessed by you and your classmates. What is your class pen/pencil total? For what percent of the class pen/pencil total does your pen/pencil account?

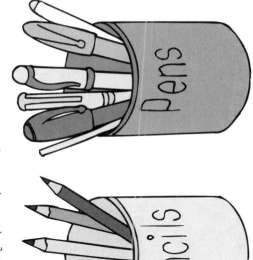

Answer Key

1. My son, Patrick, has 3 pens and 5 pencils in his desk.

2. His classmate Pauline has the most pens. She has 13 pens. Patrick has 10 pens less than Pauline. [13 - 3 = 10]

3. Melissa has the most pencils. She has 19 pencils. Patrick has 14 less pens than Melissa. [19 - 5 = 14]

4. In total, Patrick and his classmates have 117 pens.

5. Patrick's pen collection accounts for three (3) percent of the class pen total. [3 pens (Patrick) / 117 pens (class) x 100 = 2.6 = 3%]

6. In total, Patrick and his classmates have 142 pencils.

7. Patrick's pencil collection accounts for four (4) percent of the class pencil total. [5 pencils (Patrick) / 142 pencils (class) x 100 = 3.5 = 4%]

8. There are 27 students in Patrick's class. The average number of pens per person in Patrick's class is four (4). [117 pens / 27 kids = 4.3 = 4] Patrick's pen collection of three (3) numbers one (1) less than the class average of four (4) pens per person.

9. The average number of pencils per person in Patrick's class is five (5). [142 pencils / 27 kids = 5.3 = 5] Patrick's pencil collection equals the class average of five (5) pencils per person.

10. The total number of pens and pencils possessed by Patrick and his classmates is 259. Patrick's pen/pencil total is eight (8). Patrick's pen/pencil collection accounts for (three) 3 percent of the class's pen/pencil total. [8 (Patrick) / 259 (class) x 100 = 3.1 = 3%]

Desk Dissectors

Look in your desk at school. Find out:
- how many pens/pencils you have in your desk;
- how many colored pencils/crayons/markers you have in your desk;
- how many textbooks you have in your desk;
- how many workbooks/binders you have in your desk; and
- how many study aids (erasers, rulers, calculators, compasses, etc.) you have in your desk.

1. How many of each item do you have in your desk?
2. How many items do you have in your desk altogether?
3. What percent of the items in your desk are pens/pencils?
4. What percent of the items in your desk are pencil crayons/crayons/markers?
5. What percent of the items in your desk are textbooks?
6. What percent of the items in your desk are workbooks/binders?
7. What percent of the items in your desk are study aids?
8. Express the number of each of the items found in your desk as a fraction of the whole. Arrange the fractions in ascending order.
9. List the number of items found in your desk in descending order. Write the list of numbers as a single numeral. What is this numeral in words? Assign a place value to each of the digits in the numeral.
10. Reverse the numeral in question 9. What is this new numeral in words? Assign a place value to each of the digits in the numeral.

Answer Key

1. Patrick has eight (8) pens/pencils; 84 colored pencils/markers; one (1) textbook; 13 workbooks/binders; and nine (9) study aids.
2. Patrick has 115 items in his desk altogether.
3. Seven (7) percent of the items in Patrick's desk are pens/pencils. [8 p/p / 115 items total x 100 = 7%.]
4. Seventy-three (73) percent of the items in Patrick's desk are colored pencils/markers. [84 cp/m / 115 items total x 100 = 73%.]
5. One (1) percent of the items in Patrick's desk are textbooks. [1 t / 115 items total x 100 = 1%.]
6. Eleven (11) percent of the items in Patrick's desk are workbooks/binders. [13 w/b / 115 items total x 100 = 11.3 = 11%.]
7. Eight (8) percent of the items in Patrick's desk are study aids. [9 sa / 115 items total x 100 = 7.8 = 8%.]
8. The number of each of the items found in Patrick's desk expressed as a fraction of the whole and in ascending order are: textbooks = 1/115; pens/pencils = 8/115; study aids = 9/115; workbooks/binders = 13/115; and colored pencils/markers = 84/115.
9. The number of items found in Patrick's desk are, in descending order: 84, 13, 9, 8, 1. Written as a single numeral, this list is 8,413,981. In words, this numeral is eight million, four hundred thirteen thousand, nine hundred eighty-one. With place value assigned to each digit: 8 millions, 4 hundred thousands, 1 ten thousand, 3 thousands, 9 hundreds, 8 tens, 1 one.
10. The numeral in question 9, reversed is: 1,893,148. In words, this new numeral is one million, eight hundred ninety-three thousand, one hundred forty-eight. With place value assigned to each digit: 1 million, 8 hundred thousands, 9 ten thousands, 3 thousands, 1 hundred, 4 tens, 8 ones.

..
Activity 84

Soup Labelling

Like many schools, my kids' school is involved in exchanging labels for funds to buy supplies for our school. We are currently saving labels toward the purchase of a set of 40 science and technology videos. The complete set will "cost" us 112,000 labels.

1. Approximately how many cans of soup does your family use in one month?

2. Based on your estimate in Question #1, how many soup labels could your family pass on to your school in one year?

3. How many student families attend your school? If every student family ate as much soup as yours, how many labels could your school collect in one month?

4. How many soup labels could your school collect in one year?

5. How long would it take for your school to save up enough soup labels to buy a set of 40 educational videos?

6. How many labels does each video in the set "cost"?

7. If your school could purchase the videos individually, how many videos in the set could your school purchase in one year?

8. How many schools are in your family of schools? If each school donated the same number of labels per month as your school, how many video sets could your family of schools purchase in one year?

9. How many schools are in your school district? If each school collected as many labels each year as your school, how many labels could your school board collect in one year?

10. How many sets of 40 videos could your school district purchase in one year?

Answer Key

1. My family uses approximately seven (7) cans of soup in one month.

2. In one year, my family could pass on 84 labels to my kids' school. [7 labels/month x 12 months/year = 84 labels/yea.]

3. There are about 500 student families in attendance at my kids' school. If every student family ate as much soup as mine, our school could collect 3500 labels in one month. [7 labels/month x 500 student families = 3500 labels/month]

4. In one year, my kids' school could collect 42,000 labels. [3500 labels/month x 12 months = 42,000 labels/year]

5. It would take my kids' school three (3) years to save up enough soup labels to buy a set of 40 educational videos. [112,000 labels/set / 42,000 labels/year = 2.6 = 3 years]

6. Each video in the set "costs" 2800 labels. [112,000 labels/set / 40 videos/set = 2800 labels/video]

7. If my kids' school could purchase the videos individually, it could purchase 15 videos in one year. [42,000 labels/year / 2800 labels/video = 15 videos/year]

8. There are eight (8) schools in our family of schools. If each school donated the same number of labels per month as my kids' school, our family of schools could purchase three (3) video sets in one year. [3500 labels/month x 8 schools = 28,000/month. 28,000/month x 12 months/year = 336,000 labels/year. 336,000 labels/year / 112,000 labels/set = 3 sets/year]

9. There are 121 schools in our School District. If each school collected as many labels each year as my kids' school, our school district could collect 5,082,000 labels in one year. [42,000 labels/year/school x 121 schools = 5,082,000]

10. In one year, our school board could purchase 45 sets of videos. [5,082,000 labels/year / 112,000 videos/set = 45.4 = 45]

Hot Dog Day

It is Hot Dog Day at school and you're going to buy your lunch. It costs $1.25 for a hot dog, $1.00 for a can of pop, $.75 for a bag of chips, $.50 for a donut and $.25 for a cookie.

1. If you have three dollars to spend on lunch, what will you buy? How much will your meal cost? How much change, if any, will you receive?

2. If you have five dollars to spend on lunch, what will you buy? How much will your meal cost? How much change, if any, will you receive?

3. If your lunch budget is unlimited, what will you buy? How much will your meal cost?

4. What would your best friend like to order for lunch? If you are going to treat your best friend to lunch, how much will you have to spend on him or her?

5. Combine your order from question 1 and your friend's order from question 4. What is your total lunch bill?

6. Find out what your siblings would like for lunch. (If you don't have any siblings, imagine a couple!) What is the total of your family lunch bill, including your lunch from question 2? How much change, if any, would you receive from a $20 bill? (If your family meal costs more than $20, how much extra money would you need?

7. If your school hosts Hot Dog Day once a week, how much will it cost you to purchase your meal in question 3 for the whole month? (Assume four weeks in a month.)

8. If your school hosts Hot Dog Day once a month at school, how much will it cost to feed all the kids in your family for the school year? (Assume there are nine months in one school year and four weeks in a month.)

9. If each food item were double the price, how much would it cost to purchase your meal in question 3?

10. If your teacher buys a Hot Dog lunch for your class as an end-of-the-year treat, and if each student in your class orders your meal from question 2, how much will your teacher have to pay for lunch?

Answer Key

1. If I have three dollars to spend on lunch, I will buy two hot dogs and a donut. [$1.25 + $1.25 + $.50 = $3.00] My meal will cost exactly three dollars and I will not receive any change.

2. If I have five dollars to spend on lunch, I will buy two hot dogs, a can of pop and a bag of chips. [$1.25 + $1.25 + $1.00 + $.75 = $4.25. $5.00 - $4.25 = $.75] My meal will cost $4.25 and I will receive 75 cents change.

3. If my lunch budget is unlimited, I will buy three hot dogs, a can of pop and two bags of chips. [$1.25 + $1.25 + $1.25 + $1.00 + $.75 + $.75 = $6.25] My meal will cost $6.25.

4. My best friend would like to order two hot dogs, a can of pop, a bag of chips and a donut for lunch. If I am going to treat my best friend to lunch, I will have to spend $4.75 on her. [$1.25 + $1.25 + $1.00 + $.75 + $.50 = $4.75]

5. Combining my order from question 1 and my friend's order from question 4 yields a total lunch bill of $7.75. [$3.00 (my order) + $4.75 (my friend's order) = $7.75]

6. My kids would like: two hot dogs, a can of pop, a bag of chips, a donut and a cookie (Matthew); one hot dog, a can of pop, a bag of chips and a cookie (Patrick); a can of pop, a bag of chips, a donut and a cookie (Stephanie); and I would like two hot dogs, a can of pop and a bag of chips. Our total family lunch bill, including the cost of my lunch from question 1, is $15.00. [$1.25/hot dog x 5 hot dogs = $6.25; $1.00/can of pop x 4 cans of pop = $4.00; $.75/bag of chips x 4 bags of chips = $3.00; $.50/donut x 2 = $1.00; $.25/cookie x 3 cookies = $.75. $6.25 + $4.00 + $3.00 + $1.00 + $.75 = $15.00] I will receive $5.00 change. [$20 - $15 = $5]

7. If my school hosts Hot Dog Day once a week, it will cost me $25.00 to purchase my meal in question 3 for the whole month. [$6.25/week x 4 weeks/month = $25]

8. If my school hosts Hot Dog Day once a month at school, it will it cost $135.00 to feed me and my three children for the school year. [$15/month x 9 months/school year = $135]

9. If each food item were double the price, it would cost $12.50 to purchase my meal in question 3. [$6.25 x 2 = $12.50]

10. If my (son's) teacher buys a Hot Dog lunch for his class as an end-of-the-year treat, and if each student in his class orders my meal from question 2, it will cost his teacher $102.00 to pay for lunch. [$4.25 (my meal) x 24 kids in the class = $102.00]

Activity 86

Milk Math

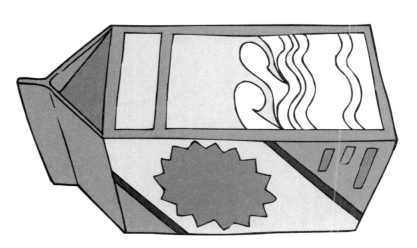

Some schools offer a lunchtime milk program. The price of a carton of milk is $.75 cents. It is possible, however, to pre-purchase milk for the month at a cost of $.50 per day. Assume there are 20 school days in a month.

1. If your family decides to purchase milk for the month ahead of time, how much will it cost to enter you and your siblings in the milk program? (If you have no siblings, consider purchasing milk for your best friend.)

2. How much money will your family save by entering the milk program over purchasing milk for each child on a daily basis for the month?

3. How much will it cost your family to enter the milk program for the entire school year?

4. In a year, how much money will your family save by entering the milk program over purchasing milk for each child on a daily basis?

5. If your family decided to purchase milk on an occasional basis, after how many days would it be more economical to enter the milk program?

6. If your sibling(s) decided not to join you in the milk program, how much would your family save over the course of a month? Assume your siblings had no milk during this period of time. Over the course of the school year?

7. If, for each day that a student is absent, the milk program refunds half of the money paid in advance, how much money would your family receive if you and your siblings each missed two days of school each week for a month?

8. If the school profits $.05/carton of milk for every student enrolled in the milk program, how much money does the school make from milk sold to your family over the course of the school year?

9. If your school offered the following family discount schedule—$.50/day for the first child, $.45/day for the second child, $.40/day for the third child, $.35/day for the fourth child, and so on—how much would it cost your family to enter the milk program for one month? How much would your family save over the course of the school year?

10. If your school offered the following family discount schedule—$.50/day for one child, $.45/day for two children, $.40/day for three or more children—how much would it cost your family to enter the milk program for one month? How much would your family save over the course of the school year?

Answer Key

1. If I decide to purchase milk for the month ahead for my seven (a slight exaggeration!) children, it will cost me $70.00 to enter them in the milk program. [7 kids x $.50/day x 20 school days/month = $70.00]

2. My family would save $35.00 by entering the milk program over purchasing milk for each child on a daily basis for the month. [7 kids x $.75/day x 20 school days/month = $105.00. $105.00 - $70.00 = $35.00]

3. It will cost my family $630.00 to enter the milk program for the entire school year. [$70.00/month x 9 months/school year = $630.00]

4. In a year, my family will save $315.00 by entering the milk program over purchasing milk for each child on a daily basis. [$35.00 savings/month x 9 months/school year = $315.00]

5. If my family decided to purchase milk on an occasional basis, it would be more economical to enter the milk program after 13 days. [7 kids x $.75/day = $5.25/day. $70.00 (milk program) / $5.25/day (occasional) = 13.3 = 13 days]

6. If only one of my seven children joined the milk program, I would save $60.00 over the course of a month [$.50/day x 20 days/month = $10.00/month. $70.00/month (all) - $10.00/month (one) = $60.00] and $540.00 over the course of the school year. [$10.00/month x 9 months/school year = $90.00. $630/year (all) - $90.00 (one) = $540.00]

7. If the milk program refunds half of the money paid in advance for every day that a student is absent, and my seven children each miss two days of school every week for a month, I will receive a $14.00 refund. [$.50 x ½ = $.25. 2 days/week x 4 weeks = 8 days. $.25 x 7 kids x 8 days = $14.00]

8. If the school profits $.05/carton of milk for every student enrolled in the milk program, the school makes $1260 from milk sold to my family over the course of the school year. [20 days/cartons/month x 7 students x 9 months/year = 1260 cartons/year. 1260 cartons/year x $.05/carton = $63.00]

9. If our school offered the following family discount schedule - $.50/day for the first child, $.45/day for the second child, $.40/day for the third child, $.35/day for the fourth child, and so on-it would cost my family $49.00 to enter the milk program for one month. [$.50 x 20 = $10. $.45 x 20 = $9. $.40 x 20 = $8. $.35 x 20 = $7. $.30 x 20 = $6. $.25 x 20 = $5. $.20 x 20 = $4. $10 + $9 + $8 + $7 + $6 + $5 + $4 = $49/month] My family would save $189.00 over the course of the school year. [$70/month (without discount) - $49/month (with discount) = $21 savings/month. $21 savings/month x 9 months/school year = $189 savings/year or $49/month x 9 months/school year = $441. $630/year (without discount) - $441/year (with discount) = $189/year]

10. If my school offered the following family discount schedule— $.50/day for one child, $.45/day for two children, $.40/day for three or more children—it would cost my family $56 to enter the milk program for one month. [$.40/day/child x 20 days/month = $8/month/child. $8/month/child x 7 children = $56/month] My family would save $126.00 over the course of the school year. [$56/month x 9 months/school year = $504. $630 (without discount) - $504 (with discount) = $126 savings/year or $70/month (without discount) - $56/month (with discount) = $14/month savings. $14/month savings x 9 months/year = $126 savings/year]

96

Pop "Tab"ulation

Did you know that you could buy electric wheelchairs with old aluminum pop tabs? It's true! In our region, students bring in pop tabs from home and collect them in a central location in the school. The tabs are then shipped to Pop Tab Headquarters at one of our local schools. The tabs are sold to an aluminum alloy company that melts down the tabs and sells or reuses the aluminum for the manufacture of other products. The alloy company pays Pop Tab Headquarters by the pound for the tabs based on the current trading price of aluminum on the stock market. When headquarters gets a request for a wheelchair from a resident in need, program volunteers use the pop tab money to make the purchase. In the region, the Pop Tabs for Wheels program has raised enough money to buy many wheelchairs for local residents.

1. How many cans of pop do your family members drink each week?

2. Based on your pop consumption in question 1, how many pop tabs could you collect in a one-month period?

3. Based on your pop consumption in question 1, how many pop tabs could you collect over the course of a year?

4. How many student families attend your school? How many pop tabs could your school collect each year if every student family submitted as many pop tabs as yours?

5. There are approximately 1000 pop tabs in a pound of aluminum. How many pounds of aluminum could your school salvage in a one-year period if every family matched your family's pop tab contribution?

6. Aluminum is currently trading at about $.70/pound. If the market remains stable and your school makes the contribution in question 5, how much wheelchair money could your school raise in one year?

7. How many schools are in your school district? If every school in the district submitted the same number of pop tabs as your school, how many pop tabs could your school district collect in a year?

8. How many pounds of aluminum could your school district salvage in one-year period? Into how many wheelchair dollars does this translate?

9. How many schools are in your school district? If every school in your district collected as many pop tabs as your school, how many tabs could the schools in your district collect in one year? How many pounds of aluminum is this? Into how many wheelchair dollars does this translate?

10. If the average cost of an electric wheelchair is $7500 how many wheelchairs could your school district purchase each year?

Answer Key

1. My family drinks 15 cans of pop each week.

2. We could collect 60 pop tabs in a one-month period. [15 tabs/week x 4 weeks/month = 60 tabs/month]

3. We could collect 780 pop tabs over the course of a year. [15 tabs/week x 52 weeks/year = 780 tabs/year]

4. Approximately 500 student families attend our school. If every student family submitted as many pop tabs as my family each year, our school could collect 390,000 pop tabs each year. [780 tabs/year x 500 families = 390,000 tabs]

5. If every family matched my family's pop tab contribution, our school could salvage 390 pounds of aluminum in one year. [390,000 tabs / 1000 tabs/pound = 390 pounds]

6. If the market remains stable and our school makes the contribution in question 5, we could raise $273 in wheelchair money in one year. [390 pounds x $.70/pound = $273]

7. There are eight (8) schools in our school district. If every school in our district submitted the same number of pop tabs as our school, our district could collect 3,120,000 pop tabs in a year. [390,000 tabs x 8 schools = 3,120,000 tabs]

8. Our family of schools could salvage 3120 pounds of aluminum in one year. [3,120,000 tabs / 1000 tabs/pound = 3120 pounds] This translates into $2184 wheelchair dollars. [3120 pounds x $.70/pound = $2184]

9. There are 121 schools in our school district. If every school in the district collected as many pop tabs as our school, the schools in our district could collect 47,190,000 in one year. [390,000 tabs/school x 121 schools = 47,190,000 tabs] This is 47,190 pounds of aluminum. [47,190,000 pounds / 1000 tabs/pound = 47,190.] This translates into $33,033 wheelchair dollars per year. [47,190 pounds x $.70/pound = $33,033]

10. At $7500 per chair, our school district could purchase four (4) wheelchairs each year. [$33,033 / $7500 per wheelchair = 4.4 = 4 wheelchairs]

Lending Library

Go to your school library and find out:

1. How many books are in circulation?
2. How many books are signed out each week? Each month? How many books are signed out over the course of a school year?
3. Based on your calculations in question 2, what percent of the school library's book collection is signed out each week? Each month? Each year?
4. How many books do you currently have on loan from your school library? For what percent of the total number of books in circulation does your current library loan account? Approximately how many books do you borrow each month from your school library? For what percent of the total monthly library loan does your monthly loan account?
5. If each student in your class borrows as many books as you do each month, how many books remain in circulation for other students?
6. How many books do you borrow over the course of a school year? For what percent of the total number of books in circulation does your annual library loan account?
7. If each student in your class borrows as many books as you do over the course of the school year as you do, how many books would your class borrow in one school year? For what percent of the total annual library loan does your class's annual loan account?
8. If every student in your school borrows as many books as you do over the course of a school year, how many books do the kids in your school borrow in one school year?

9. How many books were missing from the school library at the end of the last school year? How many missing books were returned to the library at the beginning of this school year? If the missing books cost an average of $15.00, how much money do the students in your school owe your school library?
10. If each student in your school donated two books to the school library, by how much would the school's library collection grow? By what percent would the school's library collection grow? What would be the number of books in circulation after the donation?

Answer Key

1. There are 20,000 books in circulation in my son's school library.

2. Approximately 500 books are signed out each week, 2000 each month [500 books/week x 4 weeks/month = 2000] and 18,000 each school year. [2000 books/month x 9 months/school year = 18,000]

3. Based on my calculations in question 2, 2.5 percent of the school library's book collection is signed out each week, [500 / 20,000 x 100 = 2.5%], 10 percent is signed out each month [2000 / 20,000 x 100 = 10%], and 90 percent is signed out each year [18,000 / 20,000 x 100 = 90%].

4. My son currently has one (1) book on loan from the school library. His current library loan accounts for .005 percent of the books in circulation. [1 / 20,000 x 100 = .005%] My son borrows approximately 3 books each month from the school library. His monthly library loan accounts for 0.15 percent of the total number of books borrowed from the library each month. [3 my son's monthly loan / 2000 total monthly loan x 100 = 0.15%]

5. If each student in my son's class borrows as many books as he does each month, 19,928 books remain in circulation for other students. [3 books/month x 24 students = 72 books/month. 20,000 - 72 = 19,928]

6. My son borrows approximately 27 books over the course of a school year. [3 books/month x 9 months/school year = 27 books/school year.] His annual library loan accounts for 0.14 percent of the total number of books in circulation. [27 / 20,000 x 100 = 0.135 = 0.14%]

7. If each student in my son's class borrows as many books as he does over the course of the school year, his class would borrow 648 books in one school year. [27 books/year x 24 students = 648 books. My son's class's annual loan accounts for four (4) percent of the library's total annual loan. [648 / 18,000 x 100 = 3.6 = 4%]

8. If every student in my son's school borrows as many books as he does over the course of a school year, the kids in his school borrow 20,250 books in one school year. [27 books/school year x 750 kids = 20,250]

9. There were 2000 books missing from the school library at the end of the last school year. One thousand (1000) of the missing books were returned at the beginning of this school year. If the missing books cost an average of $15.00, the students in my son's school owe the school library $15,000.00. [2000 missing books - 1000 returned books = 1000 missing books. 1000 missing books x $15/book = $15,000]

10. If each student in my son's school donated two books to the school library, the school's library collection would grow by 1500 books. [750 library students x 2 books/student = 1500.] The school's library collection would grow by 7.5 percent. [1500 / 20,000 x 100 = 7.5%] The number of books in circulation after the donation would be 21,500 books. [20,000 + 1500 = 21,500]

99

TLC10269 Copyright © Teaching & Learning Company, Carthage, IL 62321-0010

Teacher Totals

1. How many female teachers are teaching at your school? How many male teachers are teaching at your school? Are there more male or female teachers teaching at your school? How many more?

2. How many teachers in total are teaching at your school?

3. What percent of the teachers at your school are female? What percent of the teachers at your school are male?

4. How many primary, intermediate and junior? Which division has the most teachers?

5. What percent of the total teaching population teaches your division?

6. How many different teachers do you have?

7. What percent of the total teaching population teaches you? Express this figure as a fraction.

8. How many female teachers teach you? What percent of the teachers that teach you are female? Express this figure as a fraction.

9. How many male teachers teach you? What percent of the teachers that teach you are male? Express this figure as a fraction.

10. How many students attend your school? What is the teacher to student ratio at your school? What is the ratio of students in your class to the total student population?

Answer Key

1. There are 19 female teachers teaching at my daughter's school. There are eight (8) male teachers teaching at my daughter's school. There are 11 more female teachers than male teachers teaching at Stephanie's school. [19 teachers (female) - 8 teachers (male) = 11 teachers]

2. There are 27 teachers in total teaching at Stephanie's school. [19 teachers (female) + 8 teachers (male) = 27 teachers]

3. Seventy (70%) percent of the teachers at Stephanie's school are female. [19 female teachers / 27 teachers total x 100 = 70.4 = 70%.] Thirty (30) percent of the teachers at Stephanie's school are male. [8 male teachers / 27 teachers total x 100 = 29.6 = 30%]

4. There are eleven (11) primary, six (6) junior and ten (10) intermediate teachers. The primary division has the most teachers: 11.

5. My daughter is in the primary division. Forty-one (41) percent of the total teaching population teaches her division. [11 primary teachers / 27 teachers total x 100 = 40.7 = 41%]

6. Stephanie has four (4) different teachers.

7. Fifteen (15) percent of the total teaching population teaches Stephanie. [4 teachers / 27 teachers total x 100 = 14.8 = 15%] Expressed as a fraction, Stephanie is taught by $4/27$ teachers.

8. Three of Stephanie's teachers are female. Seventy-five (75) percent of the teachers that teach Stephanie are female. [3 females / 4 teachers x 100 = 75%] Expressed as a fraction, $3/4$ of Stephanie's teachers are female.

9. Stephanie has one (1) male teacher. Twenty-five (25) percent of the teachers that teach Stephanie are male. [1 male / 4 teachers x 100 = 25%] Expressed as a fraction, 1/4 of Stephanie's teachers are male.

10. There are 569 students attending Stephanie's school. The student to teacher ratio is 569:27. The ratio of students in Stephanie's class to the total student population is 6:569.

Activity 90

People Power

On the way home from school today, keep two running tallies of the people you see: a male/female tally and an adult/child tally. (Don't worry if you can't keep up. Just do the best you can. You might ask a friend to help. Get her to spot or record. Or get him to take charge of one of the tallies.)

1. How many people did you see on your way home from school?

2. How many of the people you saw on your way home were male? How many were female?

3. Did you see more males or females on your way home? How many more?

4. What percent of the people you saw on your way home were male? What percent were female?

5. How many of the people you saw on your way home were adults? How many were children?

6. Did you see more adults or children on your way home? How many more?

7. What percent of the people you saw on your way home were adults? What percent were children?

8. Look out a window in your home that overlooks a street. Count how many people walk by your house in five (5) minutes.

9. Did you see more people on your way home from school or in the five (5) minutes you spent looking out your window? How many more?

10. How many people did you see in total? What percent of the total number of people that you saw did you see walking home from school? What percent of the total number of people that you saw did you see from your window?

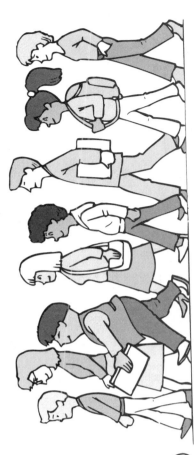

Answer Key

1. I saw 145 people driving my kids home from school today.

2. Sixty-two (62) of the people I saw on my way home were male. Eighty-three (83) of the people I saw on my way home were female.

3. I saw 21 more females on my way home than males. [83 - 62 = 21]

4. Forty-three (43) percent of the people I saw on my way home were male. [62 males / 145 people total x 100 = 42.8 = 43%] Fifty-seven (57) percent of the people I saw on my way home were female. [83 female / 145 people total x 100 = 57.2 = 57%]

5. Thirty-eight (38) of the people I saw on my way home were adults. One hundred seven (107) of the people I saw on my way home were children.

6. I saw 69 more children than adults on my way home. [107 - 38 = 69.]

7. Twenty-six (26) percent of the people I saw on my way home were adults. [38 adults / 145 people total x 100 = 26.2 = 26%] Seventy-four (74) percent of the people I saw on my way home were children. [107 children / 145 people total x 100 = 73.8 = 74%]

8. Sixteen (16) people walked by my house in five (5) minutes.

9. I saw 129 more people driving my kids home from school than I did looking out my window. [145 - 16 = 129]

10. In total, I saw 161 people. [145 + 16 = 161] I saw 90 percent of the total number of people I saw while driving my kids home from school. [145 people driving home / 161 people (total) x 100 = 90.1 = 90%.] I saw 10 percent of the total number of people I saw while looking out the window. [16 people (through window) / 161 people (total) x 100 = 9.9 = 10%]

Counting Out

Next time you are out and about, write down 10 numbers that you see in your travels.

1. Write the numbers you recorded on your trip in ascending order.

2. What is the largest number? What is the smallest number? Subtract the smallest number from the largest number. What is the difference?

3. What is the sum of the numbers? Express this number in words. Assign a place value to each digit.

4. What is the mean of the numbers? What is the median of the numbers? Compare the mean to the median.

5. Express the numbers in question 1 as a single numeral.

6. Write the numeral in question 5 in reverse.

7. Ignore the digits beyond the 100 millionth place in the numerals in questions 5 and 6. What are the new numbers? Subtract the lower of the two numbers from the higher. What is the difference? Express this numeral in words. Assign a place value to each digit.

8. Subtract the number in question 3 from the number in question 7. What is the difference? Express this numeral in words. Assign a place value to each digit.

9. Subtract the number in question 3 from the number in question 8. What is the difference? Express this numeral in words. Assign a place value to each digit.

10. Divide the numeral in question 9 by the numeral in question 3. What is the quotient? (Round your answer to the first decimal place.)

Answer Key

1. In ascending order, the numbers I recorded on my trip are: 25, 50, 74, 125, 330, 725, 505, 995, 1401 and 1599.

2. The largest number is 1599. The smallest number is 25. The difference between the largest and the smallest number is 1574. [1599 - 25 = 1574]

3. The sum of the numbers is 5829. [25 + 50 + 74 + 125 + 330 + 725 + 505 + 995 + 1401 + 1599 = 5829] In words, this number is five thousand, eight hundred twenty-nine. The place value of each digit is: 5 thousands, 8 hundreds, 2 tens, 9 ones.

4. The mean of the numbers is 583. [5829 (sum of numbers) / 10 (numbers) = 582.9 = 583.] The median of the numbers is 528. [1599, 1401, 995, 505, 725, 330, 125, 74, 50, 25. 725 (high middle number) + 330 (low middle number) = 1055 / 2 = 527.5 = 528. If the number is even, the median is half the sum of the two middle numbers.] The mean is 55 higher than the median. [583 (mean) - 528 (median) = 55]

5. The list of numbers in question 1, expressed as a single numeral, is: 25,507,412,533,072,550,599,514,011,599.

6. In reverse, the numeral in question 5 is: 99,511,041,599,505,527,033,521,470,552.

7. Ignoring the digits beyond the 100 millionth place, the new numbers in questions 5 and 6 are 514,011,599 and 521,470,552 respectively. Subtracting the lower of these numbers from the higher yields a difference of 7,458,953. In words, this numeral is seven million, four hundred fifty-eight thousand, nine hundred fifty-three. Assigning place value to each of the digits: 7 millions, 4 hundred thousands, 5 ten thousands, 8 thousands, 9 hundreds, 5 tens, 3 ones.

8. Subtracting the number in question 3 from the number in question 7 yields a difference of 7,453,124. [7, 458,953 (7) - 5829 (3) = 7,453,124] In words, this numeral is seven million, four hundred fifty-three thousand, one hundred twenty-four. Assigning a place value to each digit: 7 millions, 4 hundred thousands, 5 ten thousands, 3 thousands, 1 hundred, 2 tens, 4 ones.

9. Subtracting the number in question 3 from the number in question 8 yields a difference of 7,447,295. [7,453,124 (8) - 5829 (3) = 7,447,295] In words, this numeral is seven million, four hundred forty-seven thousand, two hundred ninety-five. Assigning a place value to each digit: 7 millions, 4 hundred thousands, 4 ten thousands, 7 thousands, 2 hundreds, 9 tens, 5 ones.

10. Dividing the numeral in question 9 by the numeral in question 3 yields a quotient of 1277.6. [7,447,295 (9) / 5829 (3) = 1277.6]

Activity 92

For Sale

On your way home from school, study (and count) the "For Sale" signs that you see on houses, buildings and building lots.

1. How many "For Sale" signs did you see on your way home from school?
2. How many of the properties were already sold? How many of the properties were still for sale?
3. What percentage of the properties were already sold?
4. What percentage of the properties were still for sale?
5. How many different real estate company signs did you see? (For the purposes of this activity, calculate each private sale by owner as a different real estate company.)
6. How many properties was the most popular real estate company offering for sale? How many properties was the least popular real estate company offering for sale? How many more properties was the most popular company offering for sale than the least popular company?
7. What percentage of the total number of signs belonged to the most popular real estate company?
8. What percentage of the total number of signs belonged to the least popular real estate company?
9. How many different real estate agents' names did you see on the signs? (Calculate each owner in a private sale as a separate agent.)
10. Did any of the agents in question 9 have more than one listing? If so, how many? What percent of the total number of properties for sale was the most popular agent listing?

Answer Key

1. Driving my son home from school today we saw 16 "For Sale" signs.
2. Two (2) of the properties were already sold. Fourteen (14) of the properties were still for sale.
3. Twelve-and-one-half (12.5) percent of the properties were already sold. [2 properties (sold) / 16 properties (total) x 100 = 12.5%]
4. Eighty-seven-and-one-half (87.5) percent of the properties were still for sale. [14 properties (for sale) / 16 properties (total) x 100 = 87.5%]
5. We saw six (6) different real estate company's signs.
6. The most popular real estate company was offering five (5) properties for sale. The least popular real estate company was offering one (1) property for sale. The most popular real estate company was offering four (4) more properties for sale than the least popular company. [5 (most popular) - 1 (least popular) = 4]
7. Thirty-one (31) percent of the total number of signs belonged to the most popular real estate company. [5 signs (most popular) / 16 signs (total) x 100 = 31.3 = 31%]
8. Six (6) percent of the total number of signs belonged to the least popular real estate company. [1 sign (least popular) / 16 signs (total) x 100 = 6.25 = 6%]
9. We saw 12 different real estate agents' names on the signs.
10. Two of the agents had multiple listings. One had four listings; the other had two listings. The most popular agent was listing 25 percent of the total number of properties offered for sale. [4 listings (most popular agent) / 16 listings (total) x 100 = 25%]

A Sign of the Times

As you are riding or walking home from school write down the numbers on every speed limit sign that you see and count the number of stop signs that you see.

1. How many speed limit signs did you see?
2. What is the sum of the numbers on the speed limit signs?
3. What is the mean speed along your route?
4. Multiply the sum of the signs by the number of speed limit signs that you saw. What is the product?
5. What was the highest speed limit that you saw? What was the lowest speed limit that you saw? What is the difference between the highest and lowest speed limit sign?
6. How many stop signs did you see?
7. Did you see more speed limit signs or stop signs? How many more?
8. What was the ratio of speed limit signs to stop signs on your trip home?
9. Combine the number of speed limit and stop signs that you saw? What is the sum?
10. Of all the signs that you saw, what percentage were speed limit signs? Of all the signs that you saw, what percentage were stop signs?

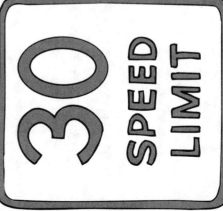

Answer Key

1. I saw 8 speed limit signs between the boys' school and home.
2. The sum of the speed signs is 300. [30 + 30 + 50 + 30 + 30 + 30 + 50 + 50 = 300]
3. The mean speed along my route is 30 miles per hour. [300 (combined speed of eight signs) / 8 (signs) = 37.5 = 38 mph]
4. Multiplying the sum of the speed limit signs by the number of speed limit signs that I saw yields a product of 2400. [300 (sum of speed signs) x 8 (speed signs) = 2400]
5. The highest speed limit that I saw was 50 mph. The lowest speed sign that I saw was 30 mph. The difference between the highest and lowest speed sign is 20 miles per hour. [50 mph (highest) - 30 mph (lowest) = 20 mph]
6. I saw 46 stop signs.
7. I saw 38 more stop signs than speed limit signs. [46 signs (stop) - 8 signs (speed) = 38 signs]
8. The ratio of speed limit signs to stop signs on my way home was 4:23. [$^8/_{46}$ / $^2/_2$ = $^4/_{23}$ = 4:23]
9. The sum of the number of speed limit signs and stop signs that I saw on my way home is 54. [8 signs (speed) + 46 signs (stop) = 54 signs]
10. Of all the signs that I saw, 15 percent were speed limit signs [8 signs (stop) / 54 signs (total) x 100 = 14.8 = 15%] and 85 percent were stop signs [46 signs (speed) / 54 signs (total) x 100 = 85.2 = 85%]

A Night at the Movies

Guess what! Your family is going to the movies!

Admission

Adults	$8.50
Students (under 18)	$7.50
Children (under 12) and Seniors (over 65)	$6.50

Food

Popcorn	Small: $2.75	Medium: $3.50	Large: $4.00
Drinks	Small: $1.75	Medium: $2.50	Large: $3.00
Candy	Small: $1.50	Medium: $2.25	Large: $3.50
Combo: Small popcorn, small drink and a small candy treat: $5.00

1. Based on the admission prices shown above, how much will it cost your family to see a movie?

2. If you have one "free admission" coupon, how will this affect the price of admission?

3. If each student and child pays five (5) dollars toward the admission price, how much of the admission tab will remain for the grown-up(s) to pay?

4. If your family is treating the next-door neighbors to a movie, how much is your two-family admission total?

5. Canvass your family to find out what food items they want to snack on during the movie. List their preferences.

6. Based on the choices in question 5, how much is your total food bill?

7. If each of your family members drops down one popcorn, drink and candy size, how much less will the food cost than question 6? (Combo and small choices remain unchanged.)

8. How much is your total "night at the movies" bill? (Use the admission figure from question 1 and food figure from question 6.)

9. If you left one person at home, by how much could your reduce your total "night at the movies" bill? What would be your new bill total?

10. If you go to the movies once a month, what will be the total of your annual "night at the movies" bill? (Use your bill total from question 8.)

Answer Key

1. Based on the admission prices shown above, it will cost my family $37.50 to see a movie. [2 (adults) x $8.50 = $17. 1 (student) x $7.50 = $7.50. 2 (children) x $6.50 = $13.00. $17.00 + $7.50 + $13.00 = $37.50]

2. If I have one "free admission" coupon, the admission price for my family will drop by $8.50 to $29.00. [$37.50 (total admission) - $8.50 (one adult admission) = $29.00]

3. If each student and child in my family pays five (5) dollars toward the admission price, my husband and I will still have to pay $22.50. [$5 x 3 children = $15. $37.50 (total admission) - $15.00 (kids' contribution) = $22.50]

4. If my family is treating the next-door neighbors to a movie, our two-family admission total will be $77.00. [3 (adults) x $8.50 = $25.50. 1 (student) x $7.50 = $7.50. 1 (child) x $6.50 = $25.50 + $7.50 + $6.50 = $39.50. $37.50 (our family) + $39.50 (neighbor family) = $77.00]

5. Jonathan: large popcorn ($4.00), large drink ($3.00), small candy ($1.50); Tracey: large popcorn ($4.00), large drink ($3.00); Matthew: medium popcorn ($3.50), large drink ($3.00), large candy ($3.50); Patrick: small popcorn ($2.75), medium drink ($2.50), large candy ($3.50); Stephanie: combo ($5.00).

6. Based on the choices in question 5, our total food bill is $39.25. [$4.00 + $3.00 + $1.50 + $4.00 + $3.00 + $3.50 + $3.00 + $3.50 + $2.75 + $2.50 + $3.50 + $5.00 = $39.25]

7. If everyone drops down one popcorn, drink and candy size, our food will cost $6.50 less than in question 6. [Jonathan: medium popcorn, medium drink, small candy ($3.50 + $2.50 + $1.50 = $7.50); Tracey: medium popcorn, medium drink ($3.50 + $2.50 = $6.00); Matthew: small popcorn, medium drink, medium candy ($2.75 + $2.50 + $2.25 = $7.50; Patrick: small popcorn, small drink, medium candy ($2.75 + $1.75 + $2.25 = $6.75); Stephanie: combo ($5.00). $7.50 + $6.00 + $7.50 + $6.75 + $5.00 = $32.75. $39.25 (total cost in question 6) - 32.75 (new total) = $6.50]

8. Our total "night at the movies" bill is $76.75. [$37.50 (admission) + $39.25 (food) = $76.75]

9. If the kids and I went to the movie together and left Jonathan at home, we could reduce our total "night at the movies" bill by $17.00. [$8.50 (admission) + $8.50 (food) = $17.00. $76.75 - $17.00 = $59.75] Our new bill total would be $59.75.

10. If we go to the movies once a month, the total of our annual "night at the movies" bill will be $921.00. [$76.75 (per month) x 12 (months/year) = $921.00/year]

Mileage Counters

1. What is the current mileage on your household vehicle? (If your family does not have a car, estimate the current miles you travel to school and back using other transportation [bus, car pool, bike, feet, etc.].)

2. Estimate the distance between your home and your school.

3. If a parent drives you to school every day, how many miles will you put on your vehicle in one week?

4. What will your odometer read after one week of driving to school?

5. If a parent drives you to school every day for a month, how many miles will you put on your vehicle? (Assume there are four weeks in a month.)

6. What will your odometer read after one month of driving to school? (Assume there are four weeks in a month.)

7. If a parent drives you to and from school every day, how many miles will you put on your vehicle in one week?

8. What will your odometer read after one week of back and forth driving?

9. If a parent drives you to and from school for a month, how many miles will you put on your vehicle?

10. What will your odometer read after one month of back and forth driving?

Answer Key

1. The current mileage on my van is 102,322 miles.

2. It is approximately 6 miles to school from our house.

3. If I have to drive my kids to school every day, I will put 30 miles on my van in one week. [6 miles/day × 5 days/week = 30 miles]

4. After one week of driving my kids to school, my odometer will read 102,352 miles. [102,322 miles (current odometer reading) + 30 miles (additional) = 102,352 miles]

5. If I drive my kids to school every day for a month, I will put 120 miles on my van. [30 miles/week × 4 weeks/month = 120 miles]

6. After one month of driving my kids to school, my odometer will read 102,442 miles. [102,322 miles (current odometer reading) + 120 miles (additional) = 102,442 miles]

7. If I drive my kids to and from school every day, I will put 60 miles on my van in one week. [30 miles/week × 2 trips/day = 60 miles/week]

8. After one week of driving kids to and from school, my odometer will read 102,382 miles. [102,322 miles (current odometer reading) + 60 miles (additional) = 102,382 miles]

9. If I drive my kids to and from school for a month, I will put 240 miles on my vehicle. [60 miles/week × 4 weeks/month = 240 miles]

10. After one month of driving my kids to and from school, my odometer will read 102,562 miles. [102,322 miles (current odometer reading) + 240 miles (additional) = 102,562 miles]

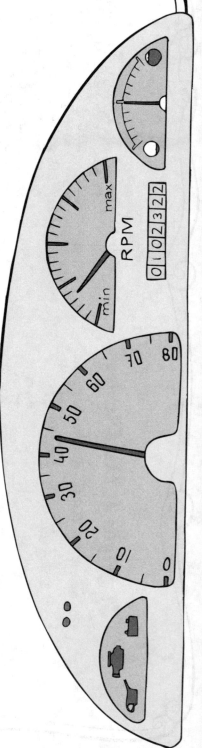

Activity 96

Home and School– and Back Again!

1. In a given month, how many times do you make the trip between home and school (and school and home)? (Assume you that you have two school days off every month: one for medical reasons and the other for holidays.)

2. Estimate the number of times you make the home-school/school-home round trip each year. (Make sure you take into account summer and Christmas holidays and spring break!)

3. How much time does each one-way trip take?

4. How much time does the round trip take every day?

5. How much time do you spend traveling to and from school each month?

6. How much time do you spend traveling to and from school each year?

7. If your round trip took twice as long, how much time would you spend traveling to and from school each year?

8. If your round trip took 1/4 as long, how much time would you spend traveling to and from school each year? How much bus time would you eliminate over the course of the school year?

9. If you were very ill and missed 1/3 of the school year, how much time would you spend traveling to and from school that year?

10. If your family decided to travel the world and took half the year off school, how much less time would you spend traveling to and from school that year?

Answer Key

1. In a given month, my kids make the trip between home and school (and school and home) 36 times. [20 school days/month - 2 absent days/month = 18 days/month. 18 days/month x 2 times = 36 times]

2. Each school year, my kids make the home-school/school-home trip 324 times. [36 times/month x 9 months/school year = 324]

3. Each one-way trip takes 25 minutes.

4. The daily round trip takes 50 minutes.

5. My kids spend 15 hours (900 minutes) traveling to and from school each month. [25 minutes/trip x 36 trips/month = 900 minutes/month. OR 50 minutes/round trip x 18 round trips = 900 minutes. 900 minutes / 60 minutes/hour = 15 hours]

6. My kids spend 135 hours traveling to and from school each year. [15 hours/month x 9 months/year = 135 hours/year]

7. If their round trip took twice as long, my kids would spend 270 hours traveling to and from school each year. [135 hours/year x 2 = 270 hours/year]

8. If their round trip took 1/4 as long, my kids would spend 33 hours, 45 minutes travelling to and from school each year. [135 hours/year x 1/4 = 33.75 hours/year. 33 hours with 0.75 hours remainder. 0.75 hours remainder x 60 minutes/hour = 45 minutes. 33 hours, 45 minutes] They would eliminate 101¼ bus hours over the course of the year. [135 hours/year - 33.75 hours = 101.25 hours each year]

9. If my kids were very ill and missed 1/3 of the school year, they would spend 90 hours traveling to and from school that year. [135 hours/year x 1/3 = 45 hours/year. 135 hours/year - 45 hours = 90 hours/year]

10. If my family decided to travel the world and took half the year off school, my kids would spend 65½ hours less time traveling to and from school that year. [135 hours/year x 1/2 = 67.5 hours/year]

Entertainment Tonight

Look at the Entertainment section of the newspaper for the movie listings.

1. How many different theaters are listed in the newspaper?

2. How many ads for different movies appear in the pages of the entertainment/movies section of the newspaper?

3. Study one of these movie ads. At how many theaters is the movie in this ad currently playing?

4. Choose one theater chain. How many different movies is that theater chain currently showing?

5. How many movies are playing at the theater (of the chain in question 2) closest to you?

6. Which theater (of the chain in question 2) is showing the most movies? How many movies is it showing? Which movie theater (of the chain in question 2) is showing the least number of movies? How many movies is it showing?

7. At the theater closest to you (see question 3), how many different ratings appear in the listings? What are these and how many movies receive each rating? What is the most popular rating at your theater right now? What is the least popular rating at your theater? Express the relative popularity of these two ratings as a ratio.

8. Of the movies showing at the theater chain from question 4, which one would you most like to see? How many theaters in the chain are currently showing this movie?

9. Assuming you could visit any theater in the chain, at any time of the day or night, what is the earliest time you could see this movie? What is the latest time you could see it? If you sat in the theater from the moment this movie first started playing until the moment the lights dimmed for the final show, how long would you have to remain in your seat? (Express in hours and minutes.)

10. How many times is the movie you most want to see playing at one theater over the weekend? (Count Friday night after 6:00 p.m.) Assuming the schedule remains the same, how many opportunities would you have to catch a weekend showing of this movie over the next month?

Answer Key

1. There are 54 different theaters listed in the newspaper.

2. There are 13 ads for different movies in the pages of the entertainment/movies section of the newspaper.

3. The movie, *Baby Day*, is currently playing at 39 theaters.

4. There are currently 48 movies showing at the ABC Theaters movie chain.

5. There are 23 different movies playing at the theater closest to me, the ABC Whitney.

6. The ABC Winston 24 and the ABC Washington 30 are tied for first place for number of movies showing. Both are currently showing 27 movies. The ABC Kennedy 20 is showing the fewest number of movies: 21.

7. The current ratings at the theater closest to me, and the number of movies with each rating, are as follows: PG13 (parental guidance) = 14; PG (parental guidance) = 8; G (general) = 1. The most popular rating at the theater closest to me is PG13. The least popular rating at the theater closest to me is G. The ratio of most popular to least popular movie ratings is 14:1.

8. The movie I would most like to see–*The Cookie Caper*–is currently playing at two (2) theaters in the chain from question 4.

9. The earliest I could see *The Cookie Caper* is at 2:00 p.m. The latest I could see this movie is at 10:35 p.m. If I sat in the theater from the moment this movie first started playing (at 2:00 p.m.) until the moment the lights dimmed for the final show (at 10:35 p.m.), I would have to remain in my seat for 8 hours and 35 minutes, or 515 minutes. [10:35 (last showing) - 2:00 (first showing) = 8 hours, 35 minutes. 8 (hours) x 60 (minutes/hour) = 480 minutes + 35 minutes = 515 minutes]

10. *The Cookie Caper*, the movie I would most like to see, is playing 12 times over the weekend. Assuming the schedule remains the same, I would have 48 opportunities to catch a weekend showing of this movie over the next month. [12 (times/weekend) x 4 (weekends/month) = 48]

Activity 98

Streetwise

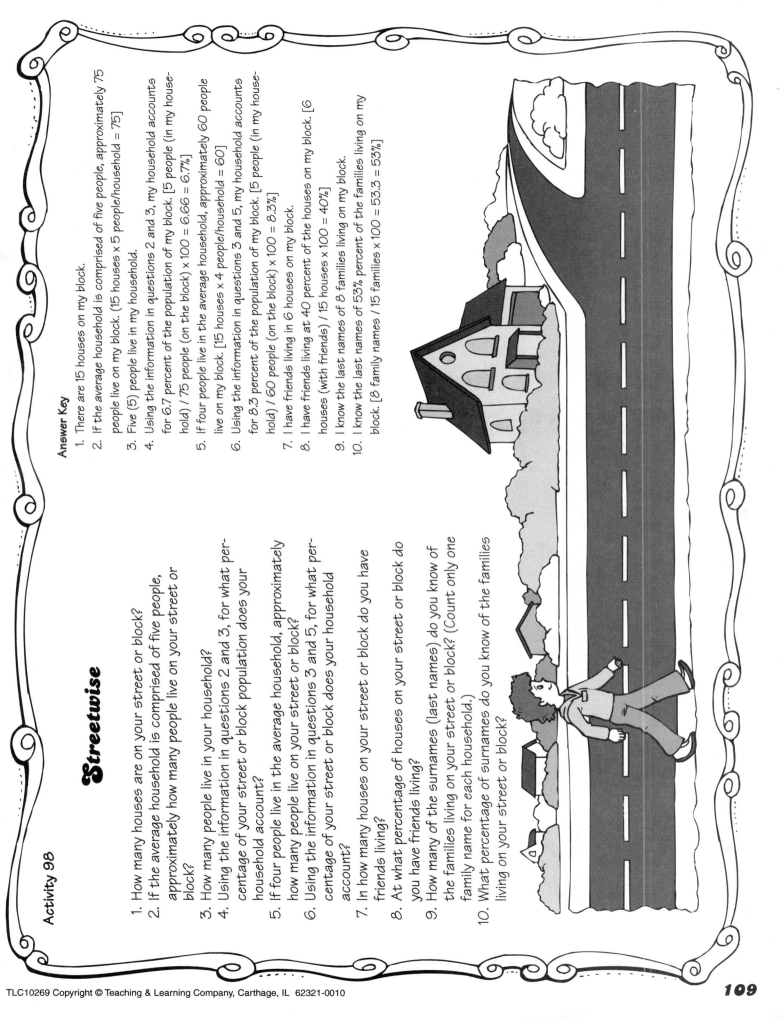

1. How many houses are on your street or block?

2. If the average household is comprised of five people, approximately how many people live on your street or block?

3. How many people live in your household?

4. Using the information in questions 2 and 3, for what percentage of your street or block population does your household account?

5. If four people live in the average household, approximately how many people live on your street or block?

6. Using the information in questions 3 and 5, for what percentage of your street or block does your household account?

7. In how many houses on your street or block do you have friends living?

8. At what percentage of houses on your street or block do you have friends living?

9. How many of the surnames (last names) do you know of the families living on your street or block? (Count only one family name for each household.)

10. What percentage of surnames do you know of the families living on your street or block?

Answer Key

1. There are 15 houses on my block.

2. If the average household is comprised of five people, approximately 75 people live on my block. (15 houses x 5 people/household = 75)

3. Five (5) people live in my household.

4. Using the information in questions 2 and 3, my household accounts for 6.7 percent of the population of my block. [5 people (in my household) / 75 people (on the block) x 100 = 6.66 = 6.7%]

5. If four people live in the average household, approximately 60 people live on my block. [15 houses x 4 people/household = 60]

6. Using the information in questions 3 and 5, my household accounts for 8.3 percent of the population of my block. [5 people (in my household) / 60 people (on the block) x 100 = 8.3%]

7. I have friends living in 6 houses on my block.

8. I have friends living at 40 percent of the houses on my block. [6 houses (with friends) / 15 houses x 100 = 40%]

9. I know the last names of 8 families living on my block.

10. I know the last names of 53% percent of the families living on my block. [8 family names / 15 families x 100 = 53.3 = 53%]

Window Watching

You will need a room with a view of the street, three pieces of paper, a pencil or pen, and a watch or clock with a second hand for this activity. (Divide each of three pieces of paper into three columns under the headings Red, White and Black.)

1. Look out a window or door at the street. Time yourself for one minute. How many cars drove by your house in one minute?

2. Repeat the trial in question 1 twice more. How many cars drove by your house in each one-minute period?

3. Find the average of your three trials in questions 1 and 2. On average, how many cars drive by your house each minute of the day?

4. Based on your average in question 3, how many cars would drive by your house in an hour?

5. Based on your average in question 3, how many cars would drive by your house in a day? A year?

6. How many cars in total drove by your house over the course of the three trials?

7. How many of the cars that drove by your house during your three trials were red? How many were white? How many were black?

8. What color car was the most popular? How many more of this color car did you count than of the other two colors?

9. What color car was the least popular? How many fewer of this color car did you count than of the other two colors?

10. Express the number of red, white and black cars as a percentage of the total number of cars you counted.

Answer Key

1. Twelve cars drove by my house in one minute.

2. In the second trial, 10 cars drove by my house. In the third trial 5 cars drove by my house.

3. The average of my three trials in questions 1 and 2 is 9. [12 + 10 + 5 = 27. 27 (total number of cars) / 3 (number of trials) = 9] On average, nine (9) cars drove by my house every minute.

4. Based on my average in question 3, 540 cars would drive by my house in an hour. [9 cars/minute x 60 minutes/hour = 540 cars/hour]

5. Based on my average in question 3, 12,960 cars would drive by my house in a day [540 cars/hour x 24 hours/day = 12,960 cars/day] and 4,730,400 cars would drive by my house in a year. [12,960 cars/day x 365 days/year = 4,730,400 cars/year]

6. In total, 27 cars drove by my house over the course of the three trial minutes. [12 +10 + 5 = 27]

7. Three of the cars that drove by my house were red, six were white and five were black.

8. White was the most popular color of car that drove by my house. I saw three more white cars than red, and one more white car than black. [6 (white) - 3 (red) = 3. 6 (white) - 5 (black) = 1]

9. Red was the least popular color of car that drove by my house. I saw three fewer red cars than white and two fewer red cars than black. [6 (white) - 3 (red) = 3. 5 (black) - 3 (red) = 2]

10. Of the cars I saw, 7 percent were red, 22 percent were white and 19 percent were black. [3 (red) / 27 (total) x 100 = 7.4 = 7% red. 6 (white) / 27 (total) x 100 = 22.2 = 22% white. 5 (black) / 27 total x 100 = 18.5 = 19% black]

Fundraising Frenzy

Think about a charitable cause for which you have helped to raise money.

1. How much money have you raised for your cause over the past year? (If you are uncertain, estimate.)

2. If everyone in your family equalled your fundraising effort in question 1, how much money could your family raise in one year?

3. If everyone in your class equalled your fundraising effort in question 1, how much money could your class raise in one year?

4. What was the average donation to your cause? (If you are uncertain, estimate.)

5. If every family on your block matched the average donation in question 4, how much money could you raise in a single fundraising drive?

6. If you set your fundraising target at $1000, and every family on your block matched the average donation in question 4, how many fundraising drives would you have to complete on your street to reach your target?

7. If half the families on your block tripled the average donation in question 4, how much money could you raise in two fundraising drives? (If there is an uneven number of families on your block, assume more families triple their donation than do not.)

8. If 14 friends joined your campaign, and each friend raised half as much as you did in question 5, how much would your group of 15 canvassers raise in a single fundraising drive?

9. If you continue to fundraise for your cause until you are 80 years old and you meet with the same success as you did in question 1, how much money will you raise between now and then?

10. If, beginning this year, the amount of money you raise doubles every 10 years, how much money will you raise by the time you are 80?

What if every person in your country matched your last year's fundraising effort? How much money could your nation raise in one year?

Answer Key

1. I have raised $75.00 for my cause over the past year.

2. If everyone in my family equalled my fundraising effort in question 1, my family could raise $375.00 in one year. [75 fundraising effort in question 1, my family members = $375.00 in one year. [75 fundraising dollars x 5 family members = $375.00]

3. If everyone in my (son's) class equalled my fundraising effort in question 1, my son's class could raise $1275.00 in one year. [$7.50 (average ing dollars x 17 students = $1275.00]

4. The average donation to my cause was $7.50.

5. If every family on my block matched the average donation in question 4, I could raise $112.50 in a single fundraising drive. [$7.50 (average donation) x 15 families = $112.50]

6. If I set my fundraising target at $1000, and every family matched the average donation in question 4, I would have to complete nine (9) fundraising drives on my street to reach my target. [$1000 target / $112.50 single drive proceeds = 8.8 = 9]

7. If half the families on my block tripled the average donation in question 4, I could raise $465.00 in two fundraising drives. [15 (families on block) / 2 = 7.5 = 8. 8 (families) x $7.50 = $180.00. 7 (families) x $7.50 = $52.50. $180 (8 families, average) + $52.50 (7 families, tripled) = $465.00]

8. If 14 friends joined my campaign, and each friend raised half as much as I did in question 5, my group of 15 canvassers could raise $900.00 in a single fundraising drive. [$112.50 / 2 = $56.25, 14 friends x $56.25 = $787.50. $787.50 (friends' contribution) + $112.50 (my contribution) = $900.00]

9. If I continue to fundraise for my cause until I am 80 years old, and I meet with the same annual success as I did in question 1, I will raise $3225.00 between now and then. [80 years (projected age) - 37 years (current age) = 43 years. 43 years x $75 dollars/year = $3225.00]

10. If, beginning this year, the amount of money I raise doubles every 10 years, I will raise $14,850.00 by the time I am 80. [37 to 47 years: 10 years x $75 = $750. 47 to 57: $75 x 2 = $150 x 10 = $1500. 57 to 67: $150 x 2 = $300 x 10 = $3000. 67 to 77: $300 x 10 = $3000. 77 to 80: $600 x 2 = $1200 x 3 = $3600. $750 + $1500 + $3000 + $6000 + $3600 = $14,850]

LC10269 Copyright © Teaching & Learning Company, Carthage, IL 62321-0010

Voluntary VIP
(Very Important Person)

Think about your role as a volunteer in society.

1. Estimate how much time you spend volunteering your services each week. (By volunteering, I mean giving freely of yourself to another without expecting anything in return. This could be a spontaneous act such as helping out Mom with dinner, or a structured activity like sorting books for the school librarian.

2. What percentage of your waking hours do you spend volunteering each week?

3. Based on your estimate in question 1, how much time do you spend in a voluntary capacity every year?

4. What is the ratio of your spontaneous voluntary time to your structured voluntary time?

5. What is the ratio of your volunteered time to your available time? (Consider school, sleep and other commitments in your answer.)

6. If you doubled your voluntary efforts, how much time could you give to others every year?

7. If you continue to volunteer your services at the same annual rate, how much time will you give to others between now and the time you are 65?

8. If everyone in your household volunteered as much time as you do in question 1, how much time would your family give to society each year?

9. If everyone in your classroom volunteered as much time as you do in question 1, how much time would your classmates give to society each year?

10. If everyone in your community gave as much volunteer time as you do in question 1, how much volunteer time could your community offer to one another each year?

If everyone in your country gave just one hour a week to others, how much volunteer time could we log each week as a nation?

Answer Key

1. I spend approximately 2 hours each week volunteering my services.

2. I spend 1.8 percent of my waking hours volunteering. [16 waking hours/day × 7 days = 112 waking hours × 52 weeks/year = 104 hours.] 112 (waking hours) × 100 = 1.78 = 1.8%.]

3. Based on my estimate in question 1, I spend 104 hours each year in a voluntary capacity. [2 hours/week × 52 weeks/year = 104 hours.]

4. I spend about one (1) hour each week doing structured volunteer work and one (1) hour each week doing spontaneous volunteer activities. The ratio of my spontaneous voluntary time to my structured voluntary time is 1:1.

5. The ratio of my volunteered time to my available time is 2:18.5. [Weekdays: Sleep: 8 hours, work: 6 hours, Mothering/domestic engineering: 6 hours, eating: 1.5 hours, exercising: 1 hour, 8 + 6 + 6 + 1.5 + 1 = 22.5. 24 hours/day - 22.5 hours = 2.5 hours free/wasted time × 5 = 12.5. Weekends: sleep: 8 hours, exercising: 1 hour, 8 + 6 + 6 + 1.5 10 hours, eating: 2 hours, mothering/domestic engineering: hours/day - 21 hours = 3 hours free/wasted time × 2 = 6. 12.5 (available weekday hours) + 6 (available weekend hours) = 18.5.]

6. If I doubled my voluntary efforts, I could give 208 hours to others every year. [2 hours/week × 2 × 52 weeks/year = 208 hours.]

7. If I continue to volunteer my services at the same annual rate, I will give 2912 hours to others between now and the time I am 65. [65 years (projected age) - 37 years (current age) = 28 years, 28 years × 104 hours/year = 2912 hours.]

8. If everyone in my household volunteered as much time as I do, my family could give 520 hours to society each year. [2 hours/week × 5 family members × 52 weeks/year = 520 hours/year.]

9. If everyone in my (son's) classroom volunteered as much time as I do, his classmates could give 2808 hours to society each year. [2 hours/week × 27 kids in class × 52 = 2808 hours/year]

10. If everyone in my community gave as much volunteer time each week as I do, our community could offer 57,200 volunteer hours to one another each year. [2 hours/week × 550 people × 52 weeks/year = 57,200 hours/year]